More Praise for The New Shape of World Christianity

"Why does much of Christian worship and witness today in Africa, Asia and Latin America resemble American Christianity? Mark Noll argues that the rising churches of the Global South and East develop 'American' forms because the social forces they encounter resemble those that shaped American Christianity. Even though thousands of American missionaries have served in these lands, local trends and needs influence the churches far more than Americans do. In making his case, Noll offers a deft overview, filled with fascinating examples, of world Christianity today. For Americans who want to learn something about Christianity as a world religion, this book is a fine place to start."
JOEL CARPENTER, NAGEL INSTITUTE FOR THE STUDY OF WORLD CHRISTIANITY, CALVIN COLLEGE

"Christians around the world rely on intellectual leaders such as Mark Noll to synthesize, challenge and propose. This book synthesizes the rising literature on global Christianity, challenges received conceptions about the American role and proposes new ways of seeing which take the issues of global reflexivity seriously. Wrapped in Noll's measured, insightful prose, this is a book which should be read by thoughtful Christians seeking to understand the most significant questions of our day."
MARK HUTCHINSON, ASSOCIATE PROFESSOR AND DEAN OF ACADEMIC ADVANCEMENT, SOUTHERN CROSS COLLEGE, SYDNEY, AUSTRALIA

"The best teachers are also learners, and this book is eloquent testimony to Mark Noll's stature as both wise teacher and continuing student. His thesis is simple: that similarity of historical conditions, rather than direct influence, is what links (white) American evangelicalism with much of non-Western Christianity today. One need not agree with all his arguments to recognize that Noll's nuanced approach is a very important counter to ideologues of both the left and the right."
VINOTH RAMACHANDRA, AUTHOR OF SUBVERTING GLOBAL MYTHS

"This fine book is one more in a long list of insightful and thought-provoking works by Mark Noll, although it gets him into new territory, that of world Christianity. Here once again is Noll's gift for deftly summarizing other scholars' findings and adding his own creative analysis to make for a stimulating product. This book is a fine antidote to the tendency toward either extreme triumphalism or self-flagellation on the issue of America's place on the world Christian scene."
DANIEL H. BAYS, PROFESSOR OF HISTORY AND ASIAN STUDIES, CALVIN COLLEGE

MARK A. NOLL

THE NEW SHAPE OF
WORLD CHRISTIANITY

How American

Experience Reflects

Global Faith

IVP Academic
An imprint of InterVarsity Press
Downers Grove, Illinois

InterVarsity Press
P.O. Box 1400, Downers Grove, IL 60515-1426
World Wide Web: www.ivpress.com
E-mail: email@ivpress.com

InterVarsity Press® is the book-publishing division of InterVarsity Christian Fellowship/USA®, a student movement active on campus at hundreds of universities, colleges and schools of nursing in the United States of America, and a member movement of the International Fellowship of Evangelical Students. For information about local and regional activities, write Public Relations Dept., InterVarsity Christian Fellowship/USA, 6400 Schroeder Rd., P.O. Box 7895, Madison, WI 53707-7895, or visit the IVCF website at <www.intervarsity.org>.

All Scripture quotations, unless otherwise indicated, are taken from the Holy Bible, New International Version®. NIV®. *Copyright ©1973, 1978, 1984 by International Bible Society. Used by permission of Zondervan Publishing House. All rights reserved.*

Design: Cindy Kiple

Images (clockwise from top left): man holding crucifix: Grant Faint/Getty Images; image used for illustrative purposes only
Chinese woman praying: Travel Ink/Getty Images; image used for illustrative purposes only
choir in Christian church: Robert Van Der Hilst/Getty Images; image used for illustrative purposes only
woman praying: AFP/Getty Images; image used for illustrative purposes only

ISBN 978-0-8308-2847-0

Printed in the United States of America ∞

Library of Congress Cataloging-in-Publication Data

Noll, Mark. A., 1946-
   The new shape of world Christianity: how American experience
   reflects global faith / Mark A. Noll.
      p. cm.
   Includes bibliographical references and index.
   ISBN 978-0-8308-2847-0 (cloth: alk. paper)
   1. United States—Church history. 2. Developing countries—Church
history. 3. Christianity—United States—Influence. 4. Missions,
American—Developing countries—History. I. Title.
   BR515.N743 2009
   270.8'3—dc22

                                                                                        2009000464

P	20	19	18	17	16	15	14	13	12	11	10	9	8	7	6	5	4	3	2	1
Y	26	25	24	23	22	21	20	19	18	17	16	15	14	13	12	11	10	09			

Dedicated to

Andrew Walls

Don Church

John Jauchen

CONTENTS

Tables and Figures

Introduction

THE NEW WORLD SITUATION FOR THE CHRISTIAN RELIGION demands a new history of Christianity. Naturally, with the startling changes that have taken place over the last century in the church worldwide, quite a bit more is needed than just a new history, especially since those changes have been as dramatic as anything experienced by the worldwide body of Christ since its very earliest years.

Older histories of Christianity remain irreplaceable; their insights are still valuable for readers with the time and energy to study them. The problem is not that earlier historical accounts are necessarily erroneous or misleading. It is rather that they presume a core Christian narrative dominated by events, personalities, organizations, money and cultural expectations in Europe and North America—and then surrounded by a fringe of miscellaneous missionary phenomena scattered throughout the rest of the globe. Such a historical picture was all but inevitable given conditions, say, in 1900 when over 80 percent of the world Christian population was Caucasian and over 70 percent resided in Europe.[1]

---

[1]David B. Barrett, Todd M. Johnson and Peter F. Crossing, "Status of Global Mission, Pres-

But today—when active Christian adherence has become stronger in Africa than in Europe, when the number of practicing Christians in China may be approaching the number in the United States, when live bodies in church are far more numerous in Kenya than in Canada, when more believers worship together in church Sunday by Sunday in Nagaland than in Norway, when India is now home to the world's largest chapter of the Roman Catholic Jesuit order, and when Catholic mass is being said in more languages each Sunday in the United States than ever before in American history—with such realities defining the present situation, there is a pressing need for new historical perspectives that explore the new world situation.

Christian theology is also being asked to address new issues that are important to the world's new Christian communities. For example, urgent questions about the place of unevangelized ancestors in the kingdom of God or about battles between angels and demons are now taking the pride of place among believers worldwide that was once given to debates concerning human free will, the changelessness of God, the subjects and mode of baptism, or the status of the papacy.

These changes now affecting all aspects of Christian life include a shifting balance in missionary activity. Today more Christian workers from Brazil are active in crosscultural ministry outside their homelands than from Britain or from Canada. More than 10,000 foreign Christian workers are today laboring in Britain, France, Germany and Italy—more than 35,000 in the United States.[2] Obviously, once-fixed notions of "sending country" and "receiving country" have been tossed into the air.

Again, the new world situation is witnessing unprecedented educational opportunities and unprecedented educational dilemmas. In the Majority World, vast numbers of eager Christian students strain thin economic resources, while in the West some well-endowed establishments are begging for students.

---

ence, and Activities, AD 1800-2025," *International Bulletin of Missionary Research* 32 (January 2008): 30.

[2]David B. Barrett, Todd M. Johnson and Peter F. Crossing, "Missiometrics 2007," *International Bulletin of Missionary Research* 31 (January 2007): 31.

Throughout the rapidly expanding Christian world—as also in the old Christian heartlands—change and changed perceptions have become the order of the day. Among many other results, the tidal wave of change is also raising important questions about how it all got this way. Thankfully, as the Guide to Further Reading at the end of this book indicates, an increasing supply of detailed writing is now becoming available for almost every part of the Christian world.

Rather than duplicating the gratifying increase of solid work on the non-Western world, this book attempts to mediate between older and newer histories. Its focus is on Christianity in the United States, but against the background of the world. For that purpose, it is vital to understand how "American Christianity" developed out of European experience, how it was transplanted to the new world, and then how it absorbed distinctive traits from the course of American experience. But the point of this book is not primarily to shed light on the history of Christianity in North America. It is, rather, to address the question of what American Christianity means for the worldwide Christian community. How, in other words, should responsible participants and observers understand the role of American Christianity in the great recent transformations of world Christianity? What has been, is and should be the relationship between Christian development in North America and Christian development in the rest of the world?

To answer that question, this book examines connections between American religious life and key developments in the recent world history of Christianity. It probes the American role in the tumultuous cascade of events that have so rapidly altered the character of worldwide Christianity. And it tries to interpret that role as both a positive and negative force. The book hopes to show why such questions are important, both because of what the United States has done in the world, but even more because of what kind of Christianity we Americans practice.

The book's major argument is that Christianity in its American form has indeed become very important for the world. But it has become important, not primarily because of direct influence. Rather, the key is how American Christianity was itself transformed when Europeans carried their faith across the Atlantic. The American model rather than

American manipulation is key. Without denying the importance of American churches, money, military might, educational institutions and missionaries for the Christian world as it is now constituted, I am suggesting that how Americans have come to practice the Christian faith is just as important globally as what Americans have done.

The chapters that follow set out this argument in some detail, but the main points can be summarized in this introduction. First, the proper start for understanding the United States in relation to world Christianity is to understand what happened in the United States itself beginning in the late eighteenth century.[3] From that point in time and over the next century one of the most successful missionary ventures of all time took place, and it took place in the United States of America (and to only a slightly lesser extent in Canada).

Second, this remarkable missionary work was accomplished through voluntary means. In North America, the older pattern of European state churches was set aside and Christian faith advanced (or declined) and flourished (or decayed) as believers took the initiative to do the work themselves. The formal and legal intermingling of church and society that had defined European Christendom for more than a thousand years faded away as a new way of organizing churches and Christian activity took its place.

Third, the type of faith that resulted when North Americans traded Christendom for voluntary Christianity was not completely different from all that had gone before. Some parallel movements in Europe have indeed shared some of the American traits, if never to the same degree.[4] Yet visitors from outside the United States have always noticed several characteristic features about the American form of Christian faith that set it apart from European forms:

---

[3]In this book it is possible only to sketch developments in American history that I have set out at greater length in *The Rise of Evangelicalism: The Age of Edwards, Whitefield and the Wesleys* (Downers Grove, Ill.: InterVarsity Press, 2003); *The Old Religion in a New World: The History of North American Christianity* (Grand Rapids: Eerdmans, 2002); and other books.

[4]David Bebbington has offered helpful reminders that qualify the sense of extreme American exceptionalism. See his essays, "Canadian Evangelicalism: A View from Britain," in *Aspects of the Canadian Evangelical Experience*, ed. George A. Rawlyk (Montreal: McGill-Queen's University Press, 1997), pp. 38-54; and "Not So Exceptional After All," *Books & Culture* (May/June 2007): 16-18.

- It was much more oriented to the Bible and the individual conscience as ultimate norms of religious authority than to tradition or history.

- It was much more pragmatic and commonsensical than formal and dogmatic.

- For successful leaders, it looked much more to entrepreneurs selecting themselves than to figures designated by a hierarchy.

- Its strong investment in the building of Christian communities relied much more on self-motivating creativity than on inherited patterns of operation.

- Its strength lay with the enterprising middle classes rather than the privileged upper classes or subservient lower classes.

- And it enjoyed an elective affinity with free-market initiatives rather than with controlled economic practice.

Fourth, it is important to remember that these American developments led to both positive and negative results. Whether they resulted in a net improvement in understanding and living out the gospel is a complex question. Some things doubtless got better. For example, by comparison with Europe, American churches witnessed much increased participation by laymen and laywomen in carrying out the tasks of the gospel. But some things doubtlessly worsened. For example, the laity and many clergy came to ignore the riches of the Christian past and the practical lessons of godliness, discipleship and effective service taught by that history. Although further evaluation of this American style is attempted at the end of the book, its main point is not evaluative but descriptive. Over the course of the nineteenth century a new style of Christianity flourished in the United States. Then—and the book is trying to underscore this latter development—over the course of the twentieth century what had become standard American religious practice grew increasingly representative of what was taking place around the world.

Finally, different explanations can be offered for why American styles of religion have become more important in the world at large. It is possible to view this development in terms of direct influence—that is, much of the rest of the Christian world now looks more and more like the Christianity in North America because North Americans have pushed it in that direction. Without denying a substantial American influence in the world, however, I will stress the advantage of seeing the newer regions of recent Christian growth as following a historical path that Americans pioneered before much of the rest of the Christian world embarked on the same path.

HOW THIS BOOK CAME TO BE WRITTEN

This book can be no more than an interim report, since what it is trying to describe is changing so rapidly. Even more, my own limited grasp of recent world history must keep conclusions provisional. Yet because of a series of influences and opportunities, I am convinced that even an interim report may stimulate other North American believers to ponder more seriously the great ongoing drama of world Christian transformation. As a reader, I have been greatly stimulated by a host of authors whose works have discerningly probed the major changes under way, especially Andrew Walls, Lamin Sanneh, Dana Robert, David Martin and Philip Jenkins.[5] I have also benefited greatly from informative personal conversations with Christian workers and Christian scholars with special knowledge about China, India, South Korea, Romania, Russia, Chad, Kenya, Nigeria, Sierra Leone, South Africa, Zimbabwe, Brazil, Nicaragua, Peru, the Philippines and the South Pacific. In addition, for several years it has been my privilege to teach a course on "the twentieth-century world history of Christianity" at Wheaton College, Regent College—Vancouver, Calvin College and the University of Notre Dame. Although I have much appreciated how students in these classes have responded to what I tried tell them, I have appreciated even more their papers, reports and experiences from around the globe. I have also been privileged to have the able assistance of my friend and coauthor Carolyn Nystrom for this project. In recent years I have been asked to write papers and deliver lectures on themes related to the new shape of world Christianity. And I have received

[5]For titles, see the "Guide to Further Reading."

articles, books, insights and much more from friends and colleagues whose generous contributions are acknowledged in the notes.

These duties, contacts and experiences have emboldened me to prepare this book. It puts to use much material that was prepared for the classroom and other assignments, but rethought and rewritten for these pages. In what follows, I am hoping to communicate to others some of the great challenges and great encouragement that I have received for my own faith from attending seriously to the new shape of world Christianity.

The book is aimed primarily at my fellow evangelical Christians, with several of the chapters focused directly on American evangelicals in relation to the world at large. There is no need to apologize for that focus, since evangelical Christianity has always been the main bridge for American believers to the non-Western world—and, with Roman Catholicism, the main religious bridge back to Europe. Still, if I could have treated the subject completely, the book would have included much more on Catholics, mainline Protestants, Eastern Orthodox, Mormons and other groups, since American representatives of these bodies also sustain rich connections to the world at large.

THE SHAPE OF THE BOOK

The central section—chapters four through seven—develops the argument that American form rather than American influence has been the most important American contribution to the recent world history of Christianity. But as a context for that contention, the first section begins in chapter two with a short sketch of the Christian world as it exists today and with a brief attempt to outline some of the challenges posed by this new reality. Then chapter three describes several developments among evangelicals during the nineteenth century that pointed in the direction of what would happen more widely in the world during the twentieth century.[6]

The second section is the heart of the volume. Chapter four first

---

[6]This chapter is revised from "Evangelical Identity, Power, and Culture in the 'Great' Nineteenth Century," in *Christianity Reborn: The Global Expansion of Evangelicalism in the Twentieth Century*, ed. Donald M. Lewis (Grand Rapids: Eerdmans, 2004), 31-51.

expands on the question about American influence in the world. Then chapter five provides a numerical history of twentieth-century missionary activity as a concrete way to chart American activity overseas. In the same vein, chapter six examines criticism that has claimed to see a controlling American hand behind modern Christian development throughout the world, and it sketches responses to that criticism. Chapter seven uses the material from the preceding chapters for returning to the main argument—that the way Christianity developed in North America during the nineteenth century has been much more characteristic of contemporary world Christianity than the older forms of European Christendom. In this second section as a whole I try to flesh out the corollary point that it is not convincing to explain the new shape of world Christianity in terms of direct American influence.[7]

The book's third section, which contains several case studies, is somewhat looser in organization. Its goal is to draw spiritual and historical lessons from the interactions of American Christianity and world Christianity. The first of these chapters examines American evangelical perceptions of the world from 1900 to 2000.[8] It surveys American evangelical magazines that were published in 1900, 1925, 1950, 1975 and 2000 in order to ask how American perceptions related to global realities. The next chapter takes up the question of what a "young church" (in this case, in South Korea) might learn from the history of Christianity in America.[9] The third case study provides an overview of the East African Revival, which began in the 1930s and continues to affect churches from the headwaters of the Nile to the southeastern African coast and in far-flung places throughout the globe. Its main point is to ask why, if so many features of this revival seem so directly related to

---

[7]This section represents an extensive rewriting and expansion of "L'influence amèricaine sur le christianisme évagélique mondial au XXe siècle," in *Le Protestantisme Évangélique: Un Christianisme de Conversion*, ed. Sébastien Fath (Turnhout, Belgium: Brepols, 2004), 59-80.

[8]This chapter is adapted from "The View of World-Wide Christianity from American Evangelical Magazines, 1900-2000," in *Making History for God: Essays on Evangelicalism, Revival and Mission In Honour of Stuart Piggin*, ed. Geoffrey R. Treloar and Robert D. Linder (Sydney: Robert Menzies College, 2004), 367-86.

[9]This chapter is adapted from a lecture to celebrate the fortieth anniversary of the Graduate School of Theology at Yonsei University, 2004, which was published in Korean to mark the event.

features of American (and European) church life, it should be considered an indigenous expression of African Christianity.[10] A short concluding chapter summarizes the book's main contentions about the great recent changes in world Christianity and then reflects on the larger meaning of these developments for believers and Christian organizations in the United States. It represents a historian's efforts to highlight the Christian meaning of the dramatic events of recent Christian history. In this last chapter, as well as at earlier points, I make use of some of the insightful things that foreign observers have had to say about the development and character of American Christianity.

                                        *   *   *

As this book was going to press, students of world Christianity were deeply saddened by the untimely death of Ogbu Kalu (1943-2009), the Henry Winters Luce Professor of World Christianity and Mission at McCormick Theological Seminary in Chicago. Ogbu's friendship, his vast learning about Christianity in Africa, his insightful guidance for historical writing on the new shape of world Christianity, and his specific insights that are used in chapter seven below—all these and more make me one of the great number who mourn his passing and thank God for his life.

The book is dedicated to three individuals who have been a special encouragement in my efforts to explore the new shape of world Christianity. Andrew Walls first opened my eyes as a historian and my mind as a Christian to the immensity of what was happening in the contemporary world. Don Church, with gentle persistence, got me to briefly set aside suburban predictability for experience on the ground in Eastern Europe, and then has remained an inspiration through the wealth of his own world Christian connections. John Jauchen, whose treasured friendship goes back more than forty years, has opened up to me the difficulties and the dilemmas, but also the nearly indescribable joy, of God's ongoing work in the non-Western world. For what these mentors have given to me this book is a meager, but heartfelt, return.

---

[10]I'm glad to acknowledge the especially helpful work of Carolyn Nystrom for this chapter.

The New Shape
of World Christianity

A GOOD WAY TO BEGIN AN INQUIRY ABOUT THE AMERICAN factor in the new shape of world Christianity is to provide a brief sketch of that new shape. And the most important thing to realize about the current situation of Christianity throughout the world is that things are not as they were. A Christian Rip Van Winkle, who fell asleep under a tree midway through the twentieth century and then woke up this past week to the sound of church bells (or a synthesizer with drums) on a Sunday morning, would not recognize the shifted shape of world Christianity. It is as if the globe had been turned upside down and sideways. A few short decades ago, Christian believers were concentrated in the global north and west, but now a rapidly swelling majority lives in the global south and east. As Rip Van Winkle wiped a half-century of sleep from his eyes and tried to locate his fellow Christian believers, he would find them in surprising places, expressing their faith in surprising ways, under surprising conditions, with surprising relationships to culture

and politics, and raising surprising theological questions that would not
have seemed possible when he fell asleep.

THE MAGNITUDE OF RECENT CHANGES

The magnitude of recent changes is the first thing, though not necessarily the most important thing, to grasp about the new world situation. A series of contrasts can underscore the great changes of the recent past:

- This past Sunday it is possible that more Christian believers attended
  church in China than in all of so-called "Christian Europe." Yet in
  1970 there were no legally functioning churches in all of China; only
  in 1971 did the communist regime allow for one Protestant and one
  Roman Catholic Church to hold public worship services, and this
  was mostly a concession to visiting Europeans and African students
  from Tanzania and Zambia.

- This past Sunday more Anglicans attended church in each of Kenya,
  South Africa, Tanzania and Uganda than did Anglicans in Britain
  and Canada and Episcopalians in the United States combined—and
  the number of Anglicans in church in Nigeria was several times the
  number in those other African countries.

- This past Sunday more Presbyterians were at church in Ghana than
  in Scotland, and more were in congregations of the Uniting Presbyterian Church of Southern Africa than in the United States.

- This past Sunday there were more members of Brazil's Pentecostal
  Assemblies of God at church than the combined total in the two
  largest U.S. Pentecostal denominations, the Assemblies of God and
  the Church of God in Christ in the United States.

- This past Sunday more people attended the Yoido Full Gospel
  Church pastored by Yongi Cho in Seoul, Korea, than attended all
  the churches in significant American denominations like the
  Christian Reformed Church, the Evangelical Covenant Church or
  the Presbyterian Church in America. Six to eight times as many
  people attended this one church as the total that worshiped in

Canada's ten largest churches combined.

- This past Sunday Roman Catholics in the United States worshiped in more languages than at any previous time in American history.

- This past Sunday the churches with the largest attendance in England and France had mostly black congregations. About half of the churchgoers in London were African or African-Caribbean. Today, the largest Christian congregation in Europe is in Kiev, and it is pastored by a Nigerian of Pentecostal background.

- This past Sunday there were more Roman Catholics at worship in the Philippines than in any single country of Europe, including historically Catholic Italy, Spain or Poland.

- This past week in Great Britain, at least fifteen thousand Christian foreign missionaries were hard at work evangelizing the locals. Most of these missionaries are from Africa and Asia.

- And for several years the world's largest chapter of the Jesuit order has been found in India, not in the United States, as it had been for much of the late twentieth century.

In a word, the Christian church has experienced a larger geographical redistribution in the last fifty years than in any comparable period in its history, with the exception of the very earliest years of church history. Some of this change comes from the general growth of world population, but much also arises from remarkable rates of evangelization in parts of Asia, Africa, Latin America and the islands of the South Pacific—but also from a nearly unprecedented relative decline of Christian adherence in Europe.

The result of population changes—in general for the world, specifically for the churches—is a series of mind-blowing realities: More than half of all Christian adherents in the whole history of the church have been alive in the last one hundred years. Close to half of Christian believers who have ever lived are alive right now. Historian Dana Robert has summarized the demographic implications with a telling statement: "The typical late twentieth-century Christian was no longer a

Table 2.1

Christian Adherence by U.N.-Defined Region (in millions)
(approximate % of population in parenthesis)

	1800	1900	2008
Africa	4.3 (4.8%)	8.8	423.7 (47.7%)
Asia	8.4 (1.4%)	20.8	355.0 (9.1%)
Europe (incl. Russia)	171.7 (91.8%)	368.2	556.4 (76.7%)
L. America	14.9 (92.0%)	60.0	530.2 (95.0%)
N. America	5.6 (35.0%)	59.6	220.4 (66.4%)
Oceania	.1 (5.0%)	4.3	22.8 (65.0%)

Source: David B. Barrett, Todd M. Johnson, and Peter F. Crossing, "Status of Global Mission, Presence, and Activities, AD 1800-2025," *International Bulletin of Missionary Research* 32 (January 2008): 30.

Table 2.2

Evangelical and Pentecostal-Charismatic Adherents (in millions)

	Evangelicals		Pentecostal-Charismatics		Ev + Pen + Ch %	
	1900	2000	1900	2000	1900	2000
Africa	1.6	69.6	.9	126.0	2.1%	25.5%
Asia	1.3	31.5	0.0	134.9	.001%	4.6%
Europe	32.4	21.5	0.0	37.6	8.1%	8.1%
L. Am.	.8	40.3	0.0	141.4	2.1%	35.6%
N. Am.	33.5	43.2	0.0	79.6	31.6%	40.0%
Oceania	2.2	4.4	0.0	4.3	36.7%	29.0%

Evangelicals = "A subdivision mainly of Protestants consisting of all affiliated church members calling themselves Evangelicals, or all persons belonging to Evangelical congregations, churches or denominations; characterized by commitment to personal religion."

Pentecostal-Charismatics = "Christian adherents belonging to identifiably Pentecostal churches and baptized members affiliated to nonpentecostal denominations who have entered into the experience of being filled with the Holy Spirit; the Second Wave of the Pentecostal/Charismatic/Neocharismatic Renewal."

Source: David B. Barrett, *World Christian Encyclopedia*, 2nd ed. (New York: Oxford University Press, 2001).

European man but a Latin American or African woman."[1] The magnitude of recent change means that all believers, including those in the former Christian heartlands of Europe and North America, are faced with the prospect of reorientation. But the scale and pace of recent developments means that more than just history needs to be reoriented; the awareness of where North American and European believers now fit within that history requires reassessment as well.

The tables on page 22 present only cold numbers, but even if they can only be "best estimates," they indicate changes of stunning proportion.

THE MULTIPLICITY OF NEW CHRISTIAN EXPRESSIONS

Almost as stunning as the magnitude of change in recent Christian history is a dramatic multiplication of the forms of Christian faith that are now found on the planet. Over the course of the last century, the Christian entrance into local cultures has accelerated as never before. Many factors have contributed to this acceleration, but the most important is translation. First came translations of the Bible into local languages, but translation has also carried liturgies, hymns, theology and devotion from the vast cultural archives of the Christian West into the emerging discourses of the world. Lamin Sanneh, an African from Gambia, was born a Muslim and as a youth memorized the Qur'an. He converted to Christianity as a young adult and then studied and taught Islamic history on several continents before taking up his current position at Yale as a professor of African studies, history and world Christianity. In a seminal book published in 1989, *Translating the Message: The Missionary Impact on Culture*, Sanneh articulated an argument that he has fleshed out considerably since that time. In his depiction, the activity of Christian translation has brought unique spiritual empowerment to those who, often for the first time, hear the message of Scripture in their mother tongues.[2] Africans, for example, are drawn into

---

[1]Dana Robert, "Shifting Southward: Global Christianity Since 1945," *International Bulletin of Missionary Research* 24 (April 2000): 50.

[2]Lamin Sanneh, *Translating the Message: The Missionary Impact on Culture* (Maryknoll, N.Y.: Orbis, 1989); and for further development, Sanneh, "Gospel and Culture: Ramifying Effects of Scriptural Translation," in *Bible Translation and the Spread of the Church*, ed. Philip C. Stine (Leiden: E. J. Brill, 1990), 1-23; *Whose Religion Is Christianity? The Gospel Beyond the West*

stories about Jesus and are not surprised when Jesus speaks to them in dreams and visions—as, according to the New Testament, he did to the early apostles.

Before 1900, portions of the Christian Scriptures had been translated into about seven hundred of the world's languages; in the past century alone, more than sixteen hundred new languages have received at least part of the Bible. Evangelical Protestants have been in the forefront of this translation effort, but Roman Catholics have not been far behind.

Results from this unprecedented effort in Bible translation have been—at one and the same time—conservative, ironic, liberating and chaotic. They have been conservative because once marginalized people are given literature in their own language, they receive a tool that anchors them to their own past, their own traditions and their own culture. One of Sanneh's key arguments is that while the spread of Islam has drawn ever-increasing numbers to the globalizing influence of Arabic, the spread of Christianity binds ever-increasing numbers to their own local languages. Ironically, although missionaries may have been very clear about what they intended when they set out to translate the Scriptures, local people have often found in their newly translated Bibles things that the missionaries did not want them to see. In one such irony, straight-laced Victorians did not realize how much unintended support they brought to the ancestral African practice of polygamy by putting the stories of patriarchs like Abraham and David into local languages.

This wave of translations has also been liberating, especially because it has given to peoples all over the world a sense of being themselves the hearers of God's direct speech. Thus, in a world where fewer and fewer can escape modern electronic technology and the reach of "imperial" languages associated with that technology—Chinese, French, Spanish and especially English—the chance to hear the Chris-

---

(Grand Rapids: Eerdmans, 2003); and *Disciples of All Nations: Pillars of World Christianity* (New York: Oxford University Press, 2008). Additional crucial insight on this same theme is provided by Andrew Walls, "The Translation Principle in Christian History," in Stine, *Bible Translation*, 24-39.

tian message in one's own mother tongue takes on even greater significance. This contrast between universal languages from outside the community and new Christian material translated into a community's traditional language makes an evangelistic tool like the *Jesus Film* from Campus Crusade for Christ extremely important. Now available in over one thousand languages and having been viewed by a total count exceeding the number of people in the world, this cinematic version of the gospel of Luke offers the first high-tech voices that many native peoples have ever heard in their own language. The fact that these voices offer the Christian story has had a transformative influence in many parts of the world.[3]

Translation, by strengthening the Christian presence in many new locations has, however, also weakened some bonds of cohesion in worldwide Christianity and pointed in the direction of religious chaos. According to David Barrett, the great enumerator of modern world Christianity, about one-fifth of the world's two billion believers are "independent," that is, not associated with the churches, denominations and traditions that have long been equated with the essence of Christianity itself.[4] This kind of independence often provides little sense of connection with past Christian wisdom or the present-day concerns of believers in other places. When new believers read the Bible in the local language within their own cultures, one of the dangers is always "syncretism," the excessive intermingling of a culture's non-Christian elements with the Christian message.

As many observers have pointed out, however, syncretism has become a difficult charge to apply with precision. It is often a question of the beholder's eye as well as what the beholder sees. Some believers in rural China may seem to incorporate a lot of ancestral superstition into their new-found faith; but such ones are also in position to ask why many Western Christians have, for example, so readily adapted themselves to the commercial Sunday, which from an orthodox Christian

---

[3]As of early July 2007, the film had been released in 1,004 languages; an audio version had been issued in over 404 languages; and a children's version was available in another 12 languages. See the Jesus Film Project official website: http://www.jesusfilm.org (accessed July 3, 2007).
[4]David B. Barrett, *World Christian Encyclopedia*, 2nd ed. (New York: Oxford University Press, 2001); plus updates in each January issue of the *International Bulletin of Missionary Research*.

perspective can look an awful lot like simply caving in to non-Christian elements of modern Western culture.

If syncretism is a danger when Christian concepts, as well as Christian books, are translated into a new culture, the translation process also says something powerful in and to the new culture. Translation implies that the receiving cultures, with their languages, histories and assumptions, are worthy of God's attention; they are valuable entities that the entrance of God's word can change into something even better.

The contemporary multiplicity of world Christianity reveals itself in a rainbow of variations throughout the world. Germany still reflects the ancient church-state establishments of Europe where a majority of the population still designates a portion of their income tax to the churches, but where only 5 to 10 percent of the people actually attend church. But among those 5 to 10 percent are some very serious believers indeed. When they are moved to evangelize the increasingly pagan populations of Europe, their first step—as a matter of built-in cultural instinct—is to form a committee. But when the same motive arises among believers in the Philippines, the first step is to just get at it. In the Philippines, organizational structures for guiding the process come later, if they come at all.

Likewise in some Christian movements among high caste Brahmins in India, strong charismatic healing ministries are present among people who refuse to organize as a church. Meanwhile, also in India believers of the Mar Thoma Church practice ancient forms of liturgy descended from the very first Christian centuries, perhaps even from Thomas, the disciple of Jesus, whom the Mar Thoma Christians look upon as their founder. Yet today there are also many congregations of Indian Mar Thoma Christians in greater Chicago and other U.S. metropolitan regions.

And so it goes in the new configuration of world Christianity, with many now deeply rooted Christian practices that do not conform to traditional Western norms:

- Some Korean Christians treat respect for ancestors—both living and dead—as a Christian duty, even though to outsiders it might look suspiciously like ancestor worship.

- In West Africa, suburban Christians on the way to the pharmacy for medication might pause to pray earnestly for divine healing—then resume the trip, fill the prescription and take the pills.

- In East Africa, a normal part of worship might include public and personal confession of sin along with repentance—a pattern growing out of the East African Revival that began in the 1930s and continues in different forms to this day.

- Meanwhile in Shanghai, members of the Local Church, or Little Flock, who are spiritual descendents of the ministry of Watchman Nee, also confess their sins to one another. Like the East African Revival, this broad stream represents local Christian appropriation of some elements of the Keswick movement, with its focus on higher spiritual life, which began in Britain in the second half of the nineteenth century.

- Brazilian television features the preaching of numerous Pentecostal preachers, who proclaim their messages in loud flamboyant tones; but also on Brazilian television are channels where Roman Catholic priests provide much the same fare.

In a word, today's Christian situation is marked by multiplicity because of how deeply the Christian message, fully indigenized in local languages, has become part of local cultures. The new shape of world Christianity offers a mosaic of many, many varieties of local belief and practice. Immigration, the modern media, global trade and the ease of contemporary travel have stirred this mixture. In many places it is possible to find traces—or more—of American influence. But the multiplicity goes far beyond what any one influence can explain, except the adaptability of the Christian faith itself.

THE MATERIAL CONDITIONS OF THE
NEW WORLD CHRISTIANITY

A subject with clear connections to the American presence in the world concerns material goods, or the realm of things that can be purchased.

The rapid diffusion of Christian adherence into parts of the world where churches barely existed 150 years ago has left a skewed distribution of resources. Today, unlike almost any other earlier period, the money and the strong educational institutions of Christianity are in one part of the world, while a majority of the active believers are located elsewhere. The result is that a Western Christian minority continues to mean a great deal for the Christian majority of the non-West. To be sure, theological education is now being offered to Nepalese in the Philippines, to Ukrainians in Romania, to West Africans in Kenya, to Latin Americans of all nationalities and traditions in Brazil, and to Chinese in Singapore. But Rome, London, Paris, Tübingen, Chicago and Boston remain destinations of choice for Christians from all over the world who seek out the highest forms of higher education.

This Western concentration of educational resources creates some odd blends of educational opportunity and inopportunity. Funding for studying the economic difficulties in modern Liberia, as an example, might be available at the University of Chicago, but probably not in Liberia. At Cambridge University, Boston University or Fuller Theological Seminary, a student wanting to study the East African Revival could find willing mentors and the possibility of fellowship support, but not as easily in Uganda and Rwanda, where such revivals actually began. As a specific example, the last few years have seen several excellent general histories of Christianity in Africa, which are cited in the "Guide to Further Reading," but not until 2005 was a thorough study produced by Africans.[5] For the most part, scholarly understanding of the world's new Christian configurations remains unbalanced. While there is a rapidly growing quantity of first-rate information-gathering for the whole world, the oversight and much of the control of that information remains with the world's established educational systems.

Another sign of global diversity is the universalization of missionary service. Sometimes this new character is a direct product of the disproportionate distribution of resources that now characterizes the world

---

[5]Ogbu Kalu, ed., *African Christianity: An African Story* (University of Pretoria: Department of Church History, 2005). This book is now available as a 2007 imprint from Africa World Press (Trenton, N.J.).

church. In Africa prior to World War II, missionaries were often the featured speakers at revival meetings that could draw several hundred Africans to a single gathering. But after the war, most revival efforts in Africa were spearheaded by Africans, with dramatically multiplied numbers and greatly altered cultural expectations. With Africans in charge, few worried about one bed per body or one chair per person. Rather, these gatherings became more like the revivals of the early American frontier where families simply made do—for transportation, for sleeping, for cooking, for seating. Africans influenced by such African-led revivals now carry to other countries their commitment to the gospel—usually first to other Africans who have left the homeland, but then increasingly to populations at large. To note comparisons over time as I try to do in chapter five is to chart the magnitude of such changes. The proportion of American, and more generally Western, missionaries in the world total of Christian missionaries is sinking fast.

But missionary funding is not the same thing as missionary recruiting. Wealth and missionary service remain connected. Even with the very rapid growth in world missionary activity, the preponderance of funding for missions still comes from the West.

What is true for missions is also true for the elusive construct called "Christian civilization." While it is impossible to define "Christian civilization" exactly, its general sense includes internalized self-discipline encouraging stable living and the postponement of immediate gratifications. It means a respect for the law, which in the West was long taken to be an objective reflection of God's righteousness. And it includes organized public support (with funds) for looking after those least able to care for themselves.

To greatly oversimplify the situation that now exists in the world, some marks of "Christian civilization" continue to persist where few people go to church while they are often absent where Christian adherence abounds. To put it graphically, if on a Sunday you want to attend a lively, well-attended, fervent and life-changing service of Christian worship, you want to be in Nairobi, not in Stockholm. But if you want to ensure that your family is well provided for if you lose your job or if you don't want to worry about how rising food prices might keep you from feeding your children, then you want to be in Stockholm, not Nairobi. In a word, the material conditions of Christianity's new world picture are opening up great opportunities, but they also pose great challenges to churches wherever they are.

POLITICAL IMPLICATIONS

The new situation of world Christianity also carries important political implications. At this level, the role of the United States as the major player in many of the world's markets, alliances and hotspots is clearly related to the movements of Christian history.

A first and most obvious implication is that both Christianity and Islam have been expanding with great rapidity precisely in those areas of the world that have been most buffeted by the forces of colonization, decolonization and now economic globalization. These terms are important enough to pause for brief definition.

Colonization refers to what took place in the expansion of Europe from early modern times (sixteenth century), with much greater intensity in the period of early industrialization (nineteenth century), and with continuing force past the mid-twentieth century. As a consequence of this expansion, much of Asia, Africa and Latin America came to be occupied, governed and economically exploited by various countries of Europe.

Decolonization took place at the end of the colonial period—for example, with the independence of India and Pakistan in 1947, the great burst of independence for African states beginning in the late 1950s and, one might say, with the triumph of Mao Tse-Tung's Communism in China in 1949.

The precipitate end of the West's direct imperial control of non-Western regions resulted in a combination of turmoil, strengthened local governments and continuing (if selective) appropriations of Western culture. Thus, for example, Kenyans speak British English and drive on the left side of the road, while across Lake Victoria to the west, Rwandans use French and drive on the right—even as most people in both nations speak several local languages and observe many local customs that straddle the new national boundaries. In China, the end of direct Western involvement in the era of Mao Tse-Tung led to massive efforts at wiping out "imperial" influence followed soon thereafter by massive efforts at appropriating selected aspects of Western capitalism. Throughout the world, the end of Western imperial rule has opened new possibilities, created new inequalities, overcome some tribal rivalries, inflamed others and—in general—accelerated the markers of social change.

Globalization refers to the process by which circulation of goods, products, money, services, movies, books, techniques, ideas and mental habits moves ever faster and easier. Even as globalization can lead to strengthened tribal identities and traditions, it almost always also draws people away from local traditions toward international practices. It is a loosely defined word used most often for economic analyses, but a word that applies just as well to the circulation of cultural ideals, practices and products as to economic ones.

Colonization, decolonization and globalization all undercut traditionally historic ways of living and thinking. Economic forces have drawn much of the world's population into new relationships. These and other tectonic historical forces have created an openness to new religious perspectives. Christianity and Islam have been the major beneficiaries. But when either Christianity or Islam moves into newly globalized regions, inevitably Muslim and Christian practices shift to meet the requirements of local settings, even as they effect change in the local settings.

Where Islam advances with Christianity in offering destabilized peoples the balm of spiritual stability—and especially where the two advance in the same or contiguous places—the potential for strife also grows. In Africa, for example, a line drawn from west to east bisecting the top third of continent would also locate some of the bitterest civil conflict of past decades; it is a line that roughly coincides with where the growing forces of Christianity and Islam meet.

The rapid spread of Christianity in economically marginal areas also poses delicate questions for those concerned about the global economy. In the great *favellas* and *barrios* of Latin America and the Philippines, as well as the teeming cities of Africa, Christian faith thrives among people whose economic existence is precarious. Sometimes that thriving comes about when Christianity is preached as a means to wealth; often it results when Christianity is embraced as a point of stability in an economically insecure world. Interpreted either way, it would seem shortsighted for policy planners to discuss economic globalization without also considering religious globalization.

But the story is different where Christianity spreads in places of economic strength, as especially in contemporary China. In this rapidly rising Asian power, the systems of belief that once guided society are passing away. Before Maoism imploded, it badly damaged ancestral reliance on Confucian precepts even as its own ineffective violence led to the suicide of communist ideology. In these circumstances, some highly educated Chinese are exploring Christianity not only for its message of personal salvation but also for its potential as a moral compass for all of society. David Jeffrey of Baylor University, who for fifteen years has been lecturing on Christian subjects at premier universities in China, has asked a speculative question that should give pause to analysts of world politics. Once before, Jeffrey observes, a great world power passed through tumultuous times as Christian ranks expanded on the margins of society. It was in the late third and early fourth centuries. In that turmoil the Emperor Constantine was converted and became, from the top of the imperial system, a supporter of Christianity as a new glue for the empire. Is it impossible to imagine that a new Constantine might exist somewhere in the junior ranks of the Chinese communist party?

The rapid spread of Christianity into new regions of the world also means that representatives from these regions will be more and more likely to bring Christian moral principles with them to international venues. Those moral principles, which emerge from Christian faith that is spreading so rapidly, are almost never liberal or modernist in either Catholic or Protestant forms. They are rather much more likely to be syncretistic, Pentecostal, strongly papal, neo-fundamentalist or starkly supernaturalist. As the worldwide Anglican Communion has experienced in its conflicts over the ordination of practicing homosexuals, the moral voice of the newer Christian regions of the world can be a strong voice indeed.[6] For the Roman Catholic Church, for ad hoc assemblages of evangelical Protestants, for older Protestant denominations, for regional and global ecumenical ventures—as also for policy analysts not focused on religion—the attachment of the world's new Christian communities to sterner interpretations of Christian faith is likely to have an ever-growing influence on international affairs.

NEW QUESTIONS FOR CHRISTIAN THEOLOGY AND PRACTICE

As much as the new shape of Christianity in the world affects general world history, much more does it influence matters of Christian belief and practice. For many in the West, such matters may have seemed mostly settled. Now, when the gospel is being appropriated by multiplying new populations—when it is being seen through new eyes—believers wherever they live have the opportunity to reconsider the priorities of doctrine. The three questions that follow hint at the challenges of theological rediscovery posed by the church's recent history around the globe, but of course there are many more.

1. How close is the world of spirits to the everyday world? In some regions it is now common for believers to recount first-hand contacts with an angel or a demon. The recent spread of Christianity has brought the supernatural and the natural much closer together than they have been in the West since the dawn of the Enlightenment. While belief in the immediate presence of God and the spirit world never died out in Western Christianity, more common for several centuries has been reliance on Bible reading, preaching and instruction of the faithful by acknowledged leaders. Yet some newly developed forms of Christianity have had little time or opportunity to develop a corpus of knowledge based on systematic inquiry into Scripture or to conform to a particular set of church authorities.

Rather, the genius of the faith in many emerging sectors of the Christian world is to merge the book of Acts with the local scene where

---

[6]See a full account in Kevin Ward, *A History of Global Anglicanism* (New York: Cambridge University Press, 2006).

the spirits are often very close. Andrew Walls reports that in his early
days as a teacher in Sierra Leone he was pushed out of his once-settled
views when he came to realize that the book of Acts was being experienced right outside his classroom door.[7] Westerners who minister in
Latin America, China, the Philippines, Africa or the South Seas consistently report that most Christian experience reflects a much stronger
supernatural awareness than is characteristic of even charismatic and
Pentecostal circles in the West. In Western Christian history there is a
long tradition of learned theological debate over cessationism—whether
or not the implementation of Christian practice based on Scripture
(Protestants), or Scripture with tradition (Catholics), has taken the
place of more direct contact with God and the spirits more generally. In
the Christian world as it exists today, that debate has been rendered
moot by a tidal wave of Christian practice. With only some hyperbole,
we might say that although some of the world's new Christian communities are Roman Catholic, some Anglican, some Baptist, some
Presbyterian and many independent, almost all are Pentecostal in a
broad sense of the term.

2. What is the unit of salvation? Protestant evangelicals usually think
that salvation is one by one by one, as individuals come to develop "a
personal relationship with Christ." But much of the emerging Christian world has not experienced conversion individually. Conversion,
instead, has taken place by families, villages or even lineages extending
back in time. Group conversion is not without historic precedent. The
great missionary to the Saxons, Boniface, regularly saw entire villages
and clans turn to Christianity during his European journeys in the
eighth century. In 1988, Russians and Ukrainians marked the 1000-
year anniversary of Christianity in their part of the world. That momentous Christian beginning took place after Prince Vladimir had
explored Islam, Judaism and Roman Catholicism before making his
choice for Eastern Orthodoxy. Then he went back to Kiev and marched
the whole city down to the river and had everyone baptized. A few
decades ago, American evangelicals could hardly imagine genuine

---

[7]Andrew Walls, *The Missionary Movement in Christian History: Studies in Transmission of Faith*
(Maryknoll, N.Y.: Orbis, 1996).

Have mennos fallen into the individuation salvation only concept?

Christian conversion taking place at the order of a prince. But today it is different. Striking examples of such conversions for whole villages and castes regularly attended the work of Bishop V. S. Azariah in India during the early decades of the twentieth century.[8] Furthermore, as experienced in India more recently among the Dalits (also known as untouchables), in Fiji, the Solomon and other islands of the Pacific, and among the families through which Christianity spreads in Korea and the Philippines—it is more and more obvious that the converting work of the Holy Spirit is not limited to individuals only.

3. How should believers read the Bible? This question can be rephrased as, what is the biblical norm by which the rest of the Bible is read?[9] A simplified list of possible keys to the whole Bible might include the narratives of the Old Testament, the Old Testament's wisdom or prophetic literature, the gospels of the New Testament, the Acts of the Apostles, the New Testament epistles or the book of Revelation. Historically in the West, the main interpretive starting points for understanding Scripture have been found in the Pauline epistles (for the Protestant reformers and many of their descendents), the Sermon on the Mount (social gospel Protestants), the Psalms (for strongly liturgical traditions), Old and New Testament prophecy (dispensationalism), and so on. Today, in much of the world it is as likely to be the narratives of Old Testament history, the Psalms (read socially and politically), the book of Acts (as direct model for contemporary action), the book of James (for its counsel about practical Christian living), or the book of Revelation (for its comfort in desperate times). To the extent that believers who use different parts of the Bible as keys to their Christian understanding talk to each other, the whole church is strengthened. To the extent they go their own way—or just shout at each other—the church is only fragmented.

A related question concerns the relevance for new Christians of the Western churches' great interpretive summaries found in the Apostles'

---

[8]Susan Billington Harper, *In the Shadow of the Mahatma: V. S. Azariah and the Travails of Christianity in British India* (Grand Rapids: Eerdmans, 2000). See also J. Waskom Pickett, *Christian Mass Movements in India* (New York: Asbury, 1933).

[9]Especially useful on this question is Philip Jenkins, *The News Faces of Christianity: Believing the Bible in the Global South* (New York: Oxford University Press, 2006).

Creed, the Nicene Creed and the Chalcedonian definition of the divine-human nature of Christ. For many believers in the West it is unimaginable that these critical statements could ever be superseded, but since they arose at specific times in Western history and in response to specifically Western problems, it is possible that they will not seem as imperative to those for whom those times and problems are foreign.

The charismatic or Pentecostal character of much of the world's new Christianity poses a yet further question. It is one that has never been completely settled in traditional Western churches, but it is absolutely front and center for most of the newer Christian regions of the world: how much are the supernatural events that fill the pages of Scripture to be considered normative examples for what happens right now? Many traditional Christians in older regions believe, and often believe quite literally, that what is related in Scripture happened pretty much as it is described, but that belief has been hedged in by centuries of structured church practice. It is not so in much of the rest of the world, where miracles, healings and prophetic words from Scripture offer a day-to-day model for contemporary Christian practice.

The printed Bible runs to hundreds of pages. No Christian has ever read every page with equal emphasis. The Puritans were theologically minded people who found themselves pondering how the epistles of Paul illuminated other sections of the Bible. Many evangelical Protestants in North America have followed roughly in the same direction. Yet these instinctive preferences are by no means the only possibilities. The Old Testament book of Leviticus is, for some African Christians today, a key to other parts of Scripture. Its legal regulations concerning holy objects, sacred days and sacred places speak directly to the cultures they have inherited. Some Asian Christians begin with the Proverbs, a biblical book that extends the search for wisdom begun in Confucian and other ancient systems of thought. Some new Christian groups turn to Paul, but via the Old Testament patriarchs whose family histories and covenantal relationships accord well with the value systems of tribal organization. For many in newly Christian regions the book of Acts is normative; it is Scripture to be followed directly and completely.

No serious theologian doubts that all believers should read and follow the teachings of Scripture. But where should they start? What sections are normative in such a way as to enlighten the rest? How should they read the Bible in its parts and the whole? Answers to these challenging questions will go far in determining the new shape of world Christianity.

*   *   *

The magnitude, the multiplicity, the material conditions, the political implications and the theological challenges of Christianity's current situation open a new epoch in religious history. This same history is also loaded with implications for world economics and world politics. Within a context of dynamic change, the United States and Christian believers in America are certainly part of the story. Attempting to define what that place has been and should be is the main purpose of this book. But before we attempt to probe this issue further, it would be wise to take a step back in time. Since hints of Christianity's new world situation were emerging in many parts of the world during the nineteenth century, it is appropriate to examine a few of those anticipations before addressing directly the question of the "American factor" today.

3

Nineteenth-Century Evangelical Identity, Power and Culture as Anticipating the Future

---

THIS CHAPTER EXPLORES THE NINETEENTH-CENTURY HISTORY of evangelical Protestants in several different parts of the world. That focus makes it possible to understand how matters of identity, power and culture that have come to characterize world Christianity in the twentieth and twenty-first centuries were taking shape in the unfolding of its "prehistory." It also allows for greater attention to the evangelical movements that, since the nineteenth century, have played such an important part in shaping the history of Christianity within the United States and also the history of American Christianity in the world at large. Moreover, what is said about evangelicals would also pertain—at different times, places and rates of developments—to other Christian traditions as well.

For a history of evangelical Christianity that takes the entire world as its domain, "the nineteenth century" can be defined as stretching from 1792 to 1910. The earlier year witnessed the publication of William Carey's *Enquiry into the Obligations of Christians to Use Means for the Conversion of the Heathens,* a landmark book that signaled the emergence of full-fledged missionary effort among English-speaking Protestants. The latter year is when the World Missionary Conference convened at the Assembly Hall of the United Free Church of Scotland in Edinburgh; this conference was the most ecumenical, most extensive and most ambitious gathering of missions-minded Protestants that had ever taken place. It came at the close of a great century of dynamic change in the world Christian picture. Although Roman Catholics, Orthodox Christians and non-evangelical Protestants certainly played large parts in that alteration, the driving forces for change were primarily evangelical. The well-considered judgments of Kenneth Scott Latourette, whose multi-volume *History of the Expansion of Christianity* is today even more relevant for world-historical concerns than when it was published over fifty years ago, are worth repeating:

> Nothing to equal [the nineteenth-century dissemination of Christianity] had been seen in the history of the faith. Nothing remotely approaching it could be recorded of any other religion at any time in the human scene. . . . [T]he nineteenth-century expansion of Christianity would not have occurred had the faith not displayed striking inward vitality. That vitality expressed itself in part through . . . revivals . . . [These revivals] were particularly marked in Protestantism. Indeed, in some respects the nineteenth century was pre-eminently the Protestant century.[1]

The dimensions of nineteenth-century Christian expansion, often evangelical Christian expansion, were stunning in their breadth, complexity and depth. In 1800 there were, according to the systematic enumerator, David Barrett, a total of one hundred Protestant foreign missionaries in the entire world.[2] For the 1910 Edinburgh Conference, the Student Volunteer Movement for Foreign Missions compiled extensive

---

[1]Kenneth Scott Latourette, *A History of the Expansion of Christianity, Vol. 6: The Great Century in Northern Africa and Asia, 1800-1914* (New York: Harper & Row, 1944), 448, 442.
[2]David Barrett, ed., *World Christian Encyclopedia* (New York: Oxford University Press, 1982), 28. Information on world population in general is from Colin McEvedy and Richard Jones, *Atlas of World Population History* (New York: Facts on File, 1978).

Table 3.1

World Population and World Christian Population: 1800, 1900, 1914

	World Pop.	*% of world Christian*	*% of Xtn. "white"*	*Total no. Xtns.*	*Total "non-white" Xtns.*	*Languages w/Scripture*
1800	900m	23.1%	86.5%	208m	28m	67
1900	1.625b	34.4%	81.1%	559m	106m	537
1914	1.8b	34.9%	76.2%	628m	149m	676

Sources: David Barrett, ed., *World Christian Encyclopedia* (New York: Oxford University Press, 1982); and Colin McEvey and Richard Jones, *Atlas of World Population History* (New York: Facts on File, 1978). "White" here equals Europe and North America; "non-white" equals Africa, Asia, Latin America and Oceania.

statistics covering "all existing foreign missionary effort which is evangelical in aim." Their survey recorded thirty-three separate regions or countries in the world where at least one hundred evangelical Protestant missionaries were at work.[3] Again according to Barrett, the proportion of the world's population that was Christian grew from about 23 percent in 1800 to almost 35 percent in 1914. This rate of growth represented the fastest proportional growth of the church since its earliest centuries—and over a period in which world population grew more rapidly than ever before. In addition, Barrett's figures suggest that the proportion of "non-white" adherents increased from slightly more than one-eighth of the Christian total in 1800 to nearly one-fourth in 1914. The combination of rapid rise in general population, proportionate expansion of Christianity, and accelerating Christian growth outside of Europe and North America meant that in 1914 the number of non-white Christians in the world was rapidly nearing the number of all Christians who were alive in 1800. Tables 3.1 and 3.2 summarize some of this information.

What these gross numbers hide are dramatic changes in many individual locations. For example, in 1910 evangelical Protestant communities of some strength existed in many parts of the world where there

[3]James S. Dennis, Harlan P. Beach and Charles H. Fahs, eds., *World Atlas of Christian Missions* (New York: SVM, 1911), 9, 83.

Table 3.2

Foreign Missionaries, Native Workers and Christian Adherents (1911)

	"foreign missionaries"	*"native workers"*	*"native Christian adherents"*
Total	21,307	103,006	6,387,736
Japan	1,029	2,138	97,117
China	4,197	1,931	470,184
India	4,635	35,354	1,471,727
All Africa	4,542	26,474	2,032,774

These figures are from 995 Protestant mission societies surveyed for the 1910 Edinburgh World Mission Conference, tabulated by location as follows: United States, 230; England, 176; India/Ceylon 85; Germany, 66; Scotland, 44; Australia, 40; Japan, 38; China, 37; South Africa, 35; Canada, 31. Source: *World Atlas of Christian Missions*, ed. James S. Dennis, et al. (New York: Student Volunteer Movement for Christian Missions, 1911).

had been no, or virtually no, Protestant presence in 1792. These places included, as an incomplete list: Japan, Korea, China, the Dutch East Indies, Melanesia, Polynesia, Australia, New Zealand, many parts of India, many regions of West Africa, East Africa, South Africa, Madagascar and Mauritius, Greenland, the United States west of the Appalachians, Canada west of Quebec, Brazil, the Lesser Antilles and Jamaica.

From 1914, the absolute expansion of Christianity, including evangelical Christianity, has continued throughout the world, although in the course of the last century that expansion has roughly matched rather than outstripped the general growth in world population. In the last one hundred years, the course of evangelical Christianity has been accelerated and complicated by two notable developments: first, the rise of Pentecostal or charismatic expressions of the faith and, second, the rise of indigenous Christian churches that may have some vestigial connections with traditional denominations but that are essentially independent. Fueled especially by Pentecostal and independent movements, Christians with more-or-less evangelical commitments are found almost everywhere on the globe. Evangelicalism, in these terms, has become a world religion of great consequence. The extraordinary expansion of the twentieth century was preceded by extraordinary expansion in the nineteenth.

EARLY EVANGELICALISM AND EUROPEAN CULTURE

Study of the nineteenth century is important for understanding the present contributions of evangelicalism to world Christianity because it was during these years that outward movement began. At the risk of oversimplification, it is useful to remember that evangelical movements emerged in the late seventeenth and early eighteenth centuries as renewal movements within state-church European Protestant regimes.[4] The leaders of these Protestant regimes saw themselves as direct descendants of the Protestant Reformation and so wanted to maintain that Reformation heritage in sharp opposition to the Roman Catholic Church. But over time, these leaders grew less concerned about the vitality of internal and lay-led church life, which was precisely the neglect that early evangelicals wanted to address.

As eager as early evangelicals were to carry out reform, their reforms were inevitably shaped by the main cultural currents of early-modern Europe. Their adaptation to these currents included a number of characteristics, most of which have strengthened in the years since:

- an innovative willingness to use the techniques of entrepreneurial market capitalism for spreading the gospel

- an eagerness to move Christian proclamation into the public spaces created by new forms of commerce and entertainment

- an assumption that the West's historic institutions of higher education could be easily and naturally exploited for evangelical purposes

- a felt need to defend the faith in terms of scientific rationality

- a countervailing concern for making the gospel relevant for an Enlightenment sense of the self

---

[4]See W. R. Ward, *The Protestant Evangelical Awakening* (New York: Cambridge University Press, 1992); and Mark A. Noll, *The Rise of Evangelicalism: The Age of Edwards, Whitefield and the Wesleys* (Downers Grove, Ill.: InterVarsity Press, 2003).

- at least the beginnings of a movement toward regarding civil society as made up of self-created and self-regulating voluntary associations

These circumstances—in which evangelical movements began— were marked by their embeddedness in the scientism, the commerce, the psychology, the Enlightenment, the education, the democratizing forces and the still dynamic Reformation consciousness of the eighteenth-century West. A survey of how that embedding took place becomes even more relevant when attention turns to later periods when non-Europeans also went about the process of embedding the Christian faith in their own cultures. The contrast between the West and the non-West is never between culture-free Christianity and culturally embedded Christianity, but between varieties of culturally embedded Christianity.

THEN AND NOW

It is much more difficult to generalize responsibly about the nature of worldwide evangelicalism today. Using conditions of the eighteenth century for comparison, however, it is possible to hazard the following tentative generalizations.

1. Worldwide evangelical movements today are much less self-conscious about the Reformation origins of Protestantism than were evangelicals in the eighteenth century. For different reasons in the West and non-West, consciousness is slight about links to Reformation leaders like Martin Luther, John Calvin, William Tyndale, Nicholas Ridley and Hugh Latimer. Similarly, the once-fixed antagonism to Roman Catholicism has fragmented—among worldwide evangelicals today can be found some continuing hostility to the Catholic Church, much indifference and some cooperation. Indeed, unlike the situation in the eighteenth century, some today who call themselves evangelicals (and who are recognized as such by others) are Roman Catholics.

2. For the most part, state-church consciousness among evangelicals has nearly vanished. Ironically, contemporary evangelicals in the United States, who in the late eighteenth century led the drive against establishment, probably look to their government for more establishment-like services today than do evangelicals in most other parts of the world.

3. For the practice of education, modern evangelicals worldwide are probably more alienated from the mainstreams of Western university life than were their predecessors in the eighteenth century. In the West, the general secularization of modern higher education has left evangelicals with a number of intellectual uncertainties, including efforts to promote an alternative science of human origins. Outside of the West the progress of the gospel has far outstripped the progress of Western higher education. The result may be that evangelicals today have more dilemmas with respect to worldly standards of knowledge than was the case two hundred years ago, but also that they possess more opportunities for educational innovation both truly Christian and truly intellectual. In addition, the burgeoning number of evangelical institutions of higher learning outside the West indicates the persistent tie between the spread of Christianity and the spread of educational aspirations.[5]

4. The connection between modern evangelicals and modern commerce has become much more complicated than was the case in the eighteenth century. In general, many evangelicals today resemble their ancestors in the faith by being flexibly entrepreneurial in using the various communication media of modern commercial capitalism. Evangelical attitudes toward the market, as opposed to the market's advanced forms of communication, however, are now widely divergent. Some modern evangelicals live in places where believers have been able to take advantage of new economic opportunities, some have been decimated by expanding markets, many are trying to gain entrance to the middle class, a few are leaders of world business, and some are vocal opponents of international free market economics. The feature of modern worldwide evangelicalism that most resembles eighteenth-century evangelicalism is that evangelicals are more inclined to action in market relationships than they are to thought about the theological meaning of markets and their effects.

5. If evangelicalism was characterized at its origins by adaptation to the

---

[5]See Joel A. Carpenter, "New Evangelical Universities: Cops in a World System, or Players in a New Game?" [two parts], *International Journal of Frontier Missions* 20 (April-June 2003): 55-65; (July-September 2003): 95-102.

*modernism of eighteenth-century Enlightenment rationalism, worldwide
evangelicalism today is radically divided among modern, postmodern and
premodern sensibilities.* Early evangelicalism featured a full measure of
premodern practices—seen most clearly in Methodist exploitation of
dreams, portents and special revelations. Yet the drift among Western
evangelicals in the late eighteenth and early nineteenth centuries was
toward modern rationalism, logocentricism and linear thought. Today,
with the prominence among evangelicals of power encounters, charismatic gifts, talismanic use of Scripture, prophecy and affectional song,
the premodern and the postmodern are probably more important in
worldwide evangelicalism than the modern. In today's evangelical
world there are many leaders eager to rationalize and dignify evangelical life and worship, but not nearly so many as there are fervent prophets and charismatic evangelists who promote a directly supernatural
orientation to all of life.

Even this inadequate glance at the journey undertaken by evangelical
movements from their origins in eighteenth-century Europe and North
America to their places throughout the world today should indicate why
attention to the nineteenth century is important. This is the period
when William Carey and the Baptist Missionary Society, the London
Missionary Society, the Church Missionary Society, the American
Board of Commissioners for Foreign Missions, and the American Bible
Society began to open up Western evangelicals to the possibilities of a
world Christianity. It was also precisely when the transition began from
what evangelical Christianity was to what it has become.

IDENTITY, POWER, CULTURE

The interrelated themes of identity, power and culture are good ones
for examining that transition. In particular, understanding how evangelicals opened up to the world offers a good opportunity to enrich
the best current definition of evangelicalism. That definition is David
Bebbington's identification of the four key marks of evangelicalism as
biblicism (a reliance on the Bible as ultimate religious authority), con-
versionism (a stress on the New Birth), activism (an energetic, individualistic approach to religious duties and social involvement) and

crucicentrism (a focus on Christ's redeeming work as the heart of essential Christianity). The 150th anniversary of the British Evangelical Alliance allowed Bebbington to restate that definition in a form useful for considering the worldwide picture: "The evangelicals across these [various] denominations are all united in the bonds of the gospel. As many of them discover, through joint expressions of their activism, . . . they all try to be obedient to the Bible and therefore faithful to the cross, and eager for conversion."[6]

Again, the theme of power is especially appropriate since the nineteenth century witnessed the move of evangelicals from their Western location—where they were either the disadvantaged struggling against the entrenched established churches or negotiators for power defined by struggle among social forces of relatively equal weight—out into the broader world. In that broader world evangelicals experienced power quite differently—many missionary evangelicals were allied or at least associated with the dominant forces of imperialistic power; by contrast, most new evangelicals in emerging churches were usually dependent in significant ways on the missionaries and were often also numbered among the least powerful in their own societies.

Culture is the most complicated of these three themes, but perhaps also the most important in any examination of the evangelical nineteenth century. In terms outlined by Andrew Walls, the incarnation of Christ provides the pattern by which the Christian faith has come to be at home (or come to be incarnated) in new cultural settings. If the essential character of Christianity is defined by Christ's incarnation in the human culture of first-century Palestine, then examining later incarnations of Christian faith in new cultures should also reveal vitally important matters about the nature of Christianity itself.[7]

A single chapter aimed at preparing the way for a consideration of

---

[6]David W. Bebbington, "Towards an Evangelical Identity," in *For Such a Time as This: Perspectives on Evangelicalism, Past, Present and Future*, ed. Steve Brady and Harold Rowdon (London: Evangelical Alliance, 1996), 46. For the original definition, see Bebbington, *Evangelicalism in Modern Britain: A History from the 1730s to the 1980s* (London: Unwin Hyman, 1989), 2-17.
[7]See especially Andrew F. Walls, "The Transmission of Christian Faith," in *The Missionary Movement in Christian History* (Maryknoll, N.Y.: Orbis, 1996), part 1.

the modern situation can make only a start on these weighty historical subjects. But it can show how issues of identity, power and cultural adaptation came to the fore as evangelical Christianity moved out from northern Europe throughout the world. In what follows I offer only two incidents out of an untold number of possibilities for each of the themes. But they should help to assess some of the important transitions of the nineteenth century that, in turn, prepared the way for the new shape of world Christianity.

IDENTITY: WHAT DID IT MEAN TO BE AN EVANGELICAL?

In 1797 an extraordinary debate took place in Sierra Leone between two exemplary evangelicals. The precipitator and recorder of the debate was Zachary Macaulay, at that time the twenty-nine-year-old governor of the colony. The son of a Church of Scotland minister, Macaulay first clerked in the office of a Glasgow merchant. Then he discovered his vocation while working as a bookkeeper on an estate in Jamaica. What Macaulay saw of slavery in Jamaica appalled him, and that disgust eventually brought him into contact with the Clapham Sect and William Wilberforce who immediately recognized his rare combination of evangelical and abolitionist zeal. From 1793 Macaulay had been serving as the assistant, and then the governor, of Sierra Leone, itself a grand experiment in evangelical philanthropy. The aim was to create on the west coast of Africa a self-sufficient colony embodying the highest ideal of Christian civilization (as defined by British experience).

The other participant, who had traversed an even more remarkable road to this encounter, was David George, in 1797 aged 54. In the early 1770s, George had been one of the founders of the black Baptist church in Silver Bluff, South Carolina, which may have been the first African American church on the North American mainland. He was converted and instructed by Particular Baptist preachers, black and white, whose view of salvation included the conservative Calvinist conviction that Christ died only—or particularly—for the elect. George himself began to exhort before he had learned to read, a skill he acquired as an adult in order to study the Scriptures. During the American Revolution, George joined the liberating British forces and continued to preach in nearby Savannah, Georgia.[8] But when the Americans defeated his liberators, he accepted transportation to Loyalist Nova Scotia where he founded the second black church to be established in that province. While in Nova Scotia, George seems to have been touched by the radical evangelicalism flowing from the ministry of Henry Alline, which combined a mystical view of God with ardent defense of human free will.[9] In 1792, after a decade in Nova Scotia, George removed to Sierra Leone with part of his congregation and became the leading black minister in that colony.

It was on April 25, 1797, that the governor, Zachary Macaulay, called George to his residence for "a free and full conversation." The result was twelve hours of talk, the gist of which Macaulay recorded in his journal. Macaulay had initiated the meeting in order to warn George away from the error of antinominaism (where Christian believers treated the law with disdain) and to convince him that holiness of life was essential for all individuals who had been truly born again by the Spirit. The conversation showed the independence of George's theology—only reluctantly did he cave in to Macaulay's barrage of Scripture texts and concede that occasional acts of drunkenness or theft were as important as Macaulay took them to be.[10] George's response to Macaulay's worry was to pose the question, "But is not God unchangeable, how then can he withdraw his love from his children?"[11] To defend his understanding of proper Christian life, George also relied much more on his own personal experiences of grace than Macaulay thought he should.

What was most interesting about Macaulay's record of the conversation, however, is his conclusion that George belonged with what he

---

[8]On George's place in the political, racial and religious history of the British occupation, see Sylvia R. Frey, *Water from the Rock: Black Resistance in a Revolutionary Age* (Princeton: Princeton University Press, 1991), 37-39.

[9]See for introduction and examples, George A. Rawlyk, ed., *Henry Alline: Selected Writings* (New York: Paulist, 1987).

[10]The conversation is summarized and excerpted in Grant Gordon, *From Slavery to Freedom: The Life of David George, Pioneer Black Baptist Minister*, Baptist Heritage in Atlantic Canada Series (Hantsport, Nova Scotia: Lancelot Press, 1992), 142-50.

[11]Ibid., 145.

called "those high Calvinists"[12] because of George's unshakable commitment to the doctrine of the perseverance of the saints, a commitment that Macaulay felt could lead only to antinomianism. Four years earlier, Macaulay recorded another incident with a similar conclusion. When a white chaplain taught that Christ's death availed for all humanity, George had rebuked him with the traditional Calvinist view that this death was intended only for the elect.[13] The intriguing thing about this debate is how difficult it was for these seasoned evangelicals to find common ground. In a faith compounded of Particular Baptist preaching, New Light experientialism, and perhaps elements of African ritual, George also incorporated elements of strongly traditional Calvinist theology. In Macaulay's moderate Calvinism, notions of civilized propriety were mingled with what he regarded as a consistent biblical ethic. George could not be convinced that Macaulay grasped the nature of Christianity as the faith that had redeemed and nurtured him. Macaulay could not grasp the vigorous theological independence that this first-generation convert from paganism was exercising in their face-to-face dialogue.

Only a few years after this debate in Sierra Leone, a series of theological disputes over a wide range of subjects took place on the American frontier. One of the main groups shaking things up included individuals who believed that the move to the frontier had rendered the traditional denominations virtually meaningless. Many of them came to be known as Restorationists.[14] This movement sought, in effect, to begin Christianity over again by stripping away the accumulated baggage of the centuries. Its name came from the effort to "restore" Christianity to the purity of the New Testament. Its leaders included a father and son who immigrated from Scotland by way of Ireland, Thomas (1763-1845) and Alexander Campbell (1788-1866). They were joined by Barton W. Stone (1772-1844), a plain-speaking Marylander who in

---

[12]Ibid., 146.

[13]Ibid., 340 n. 219.

[14]For background, see Richard T. Hughes, *Reviving the Ancient Faith: The Story of the Churches of Christ in America* (Grand Rapids: Eerdmans, 1996); and David Edwin Harrell, *Quest for a Christian America: The Disciples of Christ and American Society to 1866* (Nashville: Disciples of Christ Historical Society, 1966).

the 1790s joined the great western migration into Kentucky. The Campbells and Stone shared a disillusionment with traditional churches, which they felt were too much constrained by stale European traditions. After affiliating for brief periods with existing denominations, they eventually broke away and set about recovering the primitive Christianity they thought they had found in the New Testament's book of Acts. Alexander Campbell and Barton Stone created separate movements called "Christians only" (Stone) and "Disciples of Christ" (Campbell). The names were deliberately chosen to emphasize liberation from the historic denominations. The parallel movements were also alike in seeking to follow the New Testament literally, in practicing baptism by immersion for adult converts, and in stressing the autonomy of local congregations. In the early 1830s, the churches inspired by Stone's and Campbell's ideals joined together as the Christian Church (Disciples of Christ).

An exchange that symbolized the Restorationist disdain for tradition took place in 1811. Two of Barton Stone's associates were engaged in literary polemics with more traditional evangelicals. They were active in Kentucky, a state that in the preceding twenty years had seen its population mushroom from well under 100,000 to over 400,000. Their work was published in Cincinnati, a city on the Ohio River that had only recently sprung up out of nowhere. When Robert Marshall and J. Thompson broke into print, they left no doubt about their disdain for Protestant Christian traditions: "We are not personally acquainted with the writings of John Calvin, nor are we certain how nearly we agree with his views of divine truth; neither do we care."[15]

These incidents draw attention to questions of essential Christian identity even more than to the issue of evangelical identity. Yet in broader perspective, George and Macaulay, the Restorationists, and their opponents were all clearly evangelical. Each incident, therefore, illustrates something that happened often in the nineteenth century as evangelicals moved beyond settled locales and traditional habits. En-

---

[15]Marshall and Thompson, *A Brief Historical Account* (Cincinnati: J. Carpenter, 1811), 17. For more on this incident, see Nathan O. Hatch, *The Democratization of American Christianity* (New Haven: Yale University Press, 1989), 174.

trance into virgin territory, like the American frontier, where no Christian institutions existed to channel the energies of converts or immigrants, was often the occasion for jettisoning traditions that earlier leaders had simply taken for granted. In addition, a convert like David George, who came to faith from an environment substantially devoid of prior Christian structures, did not wait to act as a Christian until he had mastered the theological environment of the already existing evangelical world. Rather, he began his labor as a Christian thinker—as a preacher and theologian—almost as soon as he was converted. That activity as thinker, preacher and theologian was aimed, moreover, at bringing Christian resources to bear on the circumstances of the life he was living rather than at qualifying him to enter the recognized circle of established evangelical institutions.

Such activity by "new" Christians—whether Restorationists, Africans or African Americans—suggests that they were accentuating a quality present among eighteenth-century evangelicals, but a quality not highlighted in standard definitions like David Bebbington's. That quality was a willingness to set aside the authority of tradition, even evangelical tradition, in appropriating the faith for themselves. Even more than a willingness to sit lightly to tradition, it was an assumption that authoritative Christianity must set aside the baggage of its history if it was to thrive in new environments.

Some evangelicals in the late eighteenth and early nineteenth centuries leaned against Christian traditions. They were pace-setters for many worldwide evangelical ministries that have done away with Christian traditions almost entirely. In place of tradition, some evangelicals in the West, and increasing numbers outside the West, have relied upon the authority of self-created civil societies—that is, on the determination to be guided only by institutions and practices that people choose and maintain themselves. Alternatively, many evangelicals in the West, and perhaps even more outside the West, have looked to the authority of charismatic leaders. For increasing numbers of believers around the world, to embrace an evangelical form of Christianity does not represent an expression of democracy so much as a determination to follow leaders recognized for their ability to guide in the here and now. In both cases, to join the stream of evangelical Christian movements is to leave traditional authorities behind, including the authority of evangelical tradition. During the nineteenth century, worldwide evangelicalism seems to have moved steadily, and in some cases rapidly, to this understanding of self-created evangelical authority. In the years that followed, the movement grew much stronger.

WHO HOLDS THE POWER?

Two incidents from later in the century are relevant for examining questions of power—first, the struggle for unity at the 1846 London Conference of the Evangelical Alliance, and second, the stripping away of Samuel Ajayi Crowther's episcopal powers in the 1880s. Both anticipate debates and conflicts that proliferated in the twentieth century.

The 1846 London Conference of the Evangelical Alliance, which met from August 19 to September 2, was convened for the purpose of giving expression to the unity of the Church.[16] Participants came to the meeting in their capacity as individual believers, but they represented more than fifty denominations from Europe and North America. A resolution passed on the second day put the desire for unity with forceful clarity: "this Conference, composed of professing Christians of many different Denominations, all exercising the right of private judgment . . . rejoice in making their unanimous avowal of the glorious truth, that the Church of the Living God . . . is One Church, never having lost, and being incapable of losing, its essential unity. Not, therefore, to create that unity, but to confess it, is the design of their assembling together."[17] In accord with this emphasis on unity and mutual Christian love, participants labored to avoid divisive issues like whether there should be church establishments and what kind of support to give temperance movements. Delegates succeeded in formulating a nine-point basis of faith that affirmed common evangelical convictions like "(1) The Divine Inspiration, Authority, and Sufficiency of

---

[16]For research assistance on the Evangelical Alliance and on Bishop Crowther, I am pleased to thank Rachel Maxson.

[17]*Report of the Proceedings of the Conference, Held at Freemasons' Hall, London, From August 19th to September 2nd Inclusive, 1846. Published by Order of the Conference* (London: Partridge and Oakey, 1847), 44.

the Holy Scriptures. . . . (5) The incarnation of the Son of God, His work of Atonement for sinners of mankind, and His Mediatorial Intercession and Reign. (6) The Justification of the sinner by Faith alone." As it would turn out, the statement's second point posed the greatest practical difficulty: "The Right and Duty of Private Judgment in the Interpretation of the Holy Scriptures."

The one divisive issue participants could not avoid came up when they turned to the questions of permanent structures for the proposed alliance. It was the question of slavery. The difficulty arose from a stipulation, included at the urging of American delegates, that membership in any national branch of the Alliance could be automatically transferable to any other branch. British antislavery delegates feared that this stipulation would obligate them to enter into fellowship with slaveholders since the American delegation included some who owned slaves and more who were in churches that tolerated slavery.

The debate that ensued featured Britain versus the United States. The British antislavery movement, which in 1833 had secured the liberation of slaves in the British West Indies, was sympathetic to the radical wing of American abolitionism. The Rev. J. Howard Hinton of London expressed grave doubts that a man could be both a slaveholder and a Christian, since he took the biblical prohibition of "man-stealing" to mean that all slaveholding was sinful. Many of the American evangelicals were themselves personally opposed to slavery and considered it a grave evil that should be eradicated, but they did not necessarily support the demands for immediate emancipation. They pled, rather, for consideration of those slaveholders who had not chosen their situation and for whom immediate emancipation was not a viable option. The Americans were also offended by what seemed to them to be foreign meddling in a complex domestic situation from a nation with which they had so lately fought two destructive wars of independence. Americans also wondered why their particular problems were being singled out for attention when other matters embarrassing to the British were left untouched. Where, for example, was British repentance for the civil disabilities that non-Anglican Protestants continued to suffer in England?

The five days of debate—and the one hundred eighty pages in the official report—revealed unanticipated antitheses lurking in the common affirmation concerning "The Right and Duty of Private Judgment in the Interpretation of the Holy Scriptures."[18] Participants debated St. Paul's relationship to the slave owner Philemon. Others asked to add intemperance, the exploitation of children in factories and other social problems to the agenda. A member from the United States tried to define slavery as a moral issue excluded from the doctrinal basis upon which the alliance was to rest. Dr. Thomas Smyth, an Irish-born Presbyterian minister from Charleston, South Carolina, quoted the conferences' affirmation of the right of private judgment as solving the whole problem. Failing to reach an acceptable compromise on the admission of slaveholders into the alliance, the members finally decided to delay working out the details of the international organization until a future general conference—a conference that has never yet been held.

Several years after the event, Robert Baird, who spent most of his adult life in Europe as an agent for American evangelical voluntary societies, summarized American sentiments:

> The brethren from America, who were at London in 1846, returned home with heavy hearts. Some of them had been among the first, if they were not the very first, to propose the movement. They had written much about it; they had prayed much for it, and over it.... They had supposed that all who were members, in good standing, of the several evangelical branches of the one true Church of God might be received as members of this holy Alliance, with the confidence that if there were evils with which any of them were for a time entangled, and which might seem, or be under certain circumstances, inconsistent with true religion, they would be better looked after, and more certainly removed, by the proper ecclesiastical organizations, than by such an alliance as was proposed.[19]

The Americans' hopes were dashed. British evangelicals considered

---

[18]This summary of the debate is from J. B. A. Kessler Jr., *A Study of the Evangelical Alliance in Great Britain* (Goes, Netherlands: Oosterbaan & Le Cointre N.V., 1968), 44.

[19]Robert Baird, *The Progress and Prospects of Christianity in the United States of America; With Remarks on the Subject of Slavery in America; and on the Intercourse Between British and American Churches* (London: Partridge and Oakey, 1851), 42-43.

slavery more than a minor entangling evil. Concern for control over individual national destinies turned out to be stronger than shared evangelical principles. The incident showed how difficult it was to transform evangelical vitality in one place into cooperation for world expansion.

A generation after British and American differences over slavery subverted aspirations for an international evangelical association, an even more obvious power struggle played itself out in the west of Africa. Samuel Ajayi Crowther was ordained to the Anglican ministry in 1843. Then through the efforts of the Church Missionary Society's (CMS) Henry Venn, he was in 1864 appointed "Bishop of the countries of Western Africa beyond the Queen's dominion."[20] Both appointments were landmark events. To Venn, they were the culmination of his long-standing desire to see indigenous churches replace churches run from Europe. Venn's strategy of promoting self-governing, self-supporting and self-propagating African churches now seemed to be working. For his part, Crowther took on a daunting series of tasks in his Niger Mission: Bible translation, church planting, coordination of advice and funds from England, creative interaction with Muslims and recruitment of African fellow-laborers. Into the 1870s Crowther seemed to be managing this backbreaking range of duties better than any could have hoped.

But then a new generation of missionaries during a period of renewed European expansion began to express their doubts. Once begun, the expressions of doubt rolled down like thunder—in 1878, controversy between Crowther and a steamer captain sent out by the CMS to assist the work; in 1879, an audit of the Niger Mission that charged fifteen of Crowther's twenty-five managers with corruption; in 1881, a conscious decision by the CMS to extend European involvement in the mission; in 1882 and 1883, resignations and recriminations among Europeans appointed to assist Crowther; in 1883, damaging publicity in London about the murder of an African girl by two of Crowther's

---

[20]For orientation, see Andrew Walls, "Samuel Adjai (or Ajayi) Crowther," in *Biographical Dictionary of Christian Missions*, ed. Gerald H. Anderson (New York: Macmillan, 1998), 160-61; and "Samuel Ajayi Crowther, 1807-1891: Foremost African Christian of the Nineteenth Century," in *Mission Legacies*, ed. Gerald H. Anderson et al. (Maryknoll, N.Y.: Orbis, 1994), 132-39.

agents several years before; in 1886, the creation of the Royal Niger Company that created British colonial protectorates over much of Crowther's jurisdiction that had previously lain "beyond the Queen's dominions"; in 1889, the transfer of much of Crowther's remaining authority to a new "Sudan Party" of young English missionaries; in 1890, the wholesale suspension of African agents, including the Bishop's son, D. C. Crowther, for reasons involving funds and factional loyalties; in 1891, upon the death of Bishop Crowther, the appointment of an Englishman as his successor.

Details of Crowther's interaction with CMS missionaries from England are probably not the key to this incident. In world-historical perspective, Crowther's Niger Mission, along with Venn's three-self principles, were swept away by an avalanche, the European scramble for African colonies. If that avalanche was not enough, other bombardments out of Europe would have done the job—for example, the intensification of racialist understandings of history and the rise of Social Darwinism (whereby Crowther, as an African sold into slavery as a youth, represented a weak member of the least fit race).

Even in the face of these tectonic shifts, however, the development of local fault lines still deserves attention. Of those local faults, one of the most pertinent for evangelical history was the theological character of the young English missionaries who from the mid-1880s did so much to undermine Crowther's work. That theological character was formed by the newer Keswick emphasis on the Higher Life and by the growing influence of a kind of pietism that rejected Christian engagement with culture. Against Crowther's strategy of using schools and other structures borrowed from Western societies, the new missionaries pursued a "more individualistic and more otherworldly" plan. In the words of J. F. A. Ajayi, the new missionaries "itched to go into the villages and live like the 'natives' they despised, in the belief that by 'reasoning of the Gospel and righteousness' they would sweep them out of their old ways into a pure, simple, primitive Christianity."[21] Evangelical

---

[21]J. F. Ade Ajayi, *Christian Missions in Nigeria 1841-1891: The Making of a New Elite* (Evanston, Ill.: Northwestern University Press, 1969), 50. For "individualistic" and "otherwordly," see Walls, "Crowther," 137.

currents that were doubtless producing a quickening effect in the West
worked with quite different results along the Niger.

What can the stories of the 1846 London conference or of changes
in Samuel Crowther's Niger Mission tell us about evangelicals and
power? At the very least, these accounts show that evangelical spirituality, which has always had such great potential for strengthening individual Christian life, also bears a number of chronic perils. As illustrated by the failure of the Evangelical Alliance, these perils include a
naive reluctance to acknowledge differences between the ability of
Scripture to speak in every conceivable human situation and the interpretations of the Bible produced by particular social or historical locations. They also include a self-delusionary innocence about the despotic
dangers, as well as the liberating potential, of "the Right and Duty of
Private Judgment in the Interpretation of the Holy Scriptures." As illustrated by the experience of Samuel Crowther, these perils include
the capacity of Higher Life theologies to mask the continuation of
Lower Life pride and self-seeking, even among the converted. They
include as well a tendency to personalize and spiritualize the gospel to
such an extent that the influence of world historical forces drops be-
neath the horizon of conscious thought.

These incidents do testify to the power of the gospel interpreted in
evangelical terms: There would have been no attempt at an international
Evangelical Alliance if multitudes in several continents had not been
called to God by similar messages about the saving power of the cross.
There would not have been a Niger Mission to undermine if the message of redemption in Christ had not miraculously altered the life course
of many Englishmen and women and many more in West Africa. Both
incidents also testify, however, to the propensity of evangelicalism,
which promotes an intensely personal faith, to obscure broader dimensions of the gospel. Participants at the Evangelical Alliance conference
confessed their belief in "The utter Depravity of Human Nature, in
consequence of the Fall." Keswick-trained missionaries testified by their
protracted individual struggles for personal holiness that they knew sin
was not easily uprooted. But when it came to understanding how interpretation of Scripture can reflect as well as reveal power relationships,

when it came to remembering that the gospel spoke to human structures as well as to human hearts, they forgot. Nineteenth-century evangelicals made a drastic difference in the world because they believed the death of Christ had conquered the oppressive powers of sin, death, hell and the devil. They opened themselves to cheap grace when they looked upon the atonement of Christ as exempting themselves from the universal human tendency to act as oppressors.

Much of what happened among evangelicals in the nineteenth century has been repeated among Christians of many sorts throughout the world in the centuries that followed. However reluctant some Christian groups have been to talk directly about the exercise of power, power is a constant presence in the recent world history of Christianity—power as financial means, power as protected by military might, power as dominance through communications media, power through control of education, and more. No body of Christians has been as capable at exercising power as American believers, though few have been more reluctant to address questions of power face-on. The stalled debates of the Evangelical Alliance at London in 1846 and the missionary manipulations leading to S. A. Crowther's sidelining in the late 1880s offered a foretaste of other standoffs and other manipulations to come. American Christian believers have played various roles in those later developments, but they have been a major part of the American presence in the Christian world as a whole.

THE CHALLENGES OF CULTURAL ADAPTATION

During the nineteenth century, evangelical life in a multiplying number of societies was leading to a spectacular kaleidoscope of cultural permutations, adaptations, disruptions and transformations. A full cultural history of evangelical movements would be very complicated, since it would have to include developments in older Christian communities, the results of missionary efforts, the different rate of indigenization in many different locations and the maturing of belief and practice in new Christian regions.[22] What brief attention to only two

---

[22]For solid overviews, see John Wolffe, *The Expansion of Evangelicalism: The Age of Wilberforce, More, Chalmers and Finney* (Downers Grove, Ill.: InterVarsity Press, 2007); and David W.

nineteenth-century incidents can suggest, however, is that study of the past can be very useful for interpreting the present.

From insights contributed by leading historians of world Christianity—especially Ogbu Kalu, Brian Stanley and Andrew Walls—I would like to draw attention to one of the nineteenth-century events that is most pertinent for believers to contemplate in the early twenty-first century. It is the 1841 Niger Expedition of Thomas Fowell Buxton.[23] That expedition, which Buxton undertook in order to extend the evangelical battle against slavery, is widely perceived as a failure—"brief and disastrous," in Kenneth Scott Latourette's words, a "panacea," according to David Livingstone's biographer Tim Jeal, that resulted only in "heavy loss of life and little or no achievement."[24] Recent studies by Africans may be successfully revising judgments about the nature of Buxton's failure, but they do not alter the conclusion that his expensive and highly publicized expedition failed to set up the farms, trading networks and churches that he hoped would both drive slavery out of the Niger River Valley and, as a byproduct, turn a profit for all concerned.

It is not the record of this mission, and not necessarily the detailed shape of Buxton's hopes, that speak so directly to later history. It is, rather, his wisdom in joining the fortunes of Christianity, commerce and civilization into one common program. At the end of a lengthy appeal from 1840, *The African Slave Trade and Its Remedy,* Buxton waxed euphoric about the benefits he foresaw if only scientific agriculture could replace slavery as the backbone of the West African economy. As he did so, however, he paused to insist that links between a successful commercial agriculture and the advancement of civilization had to rest

Bebbington, *The Dominance of Evangelicalism: The Age of Spurgeon and Moody* (Downers Grove, Ill.: InterVarsity Press, 2005).

[23]This brief treatment relies especially upon Andrew F. Walls, "Thomas Fowell Buxton, 1786-1844: Missions and the Remedy for African Slavery," in *Mission Legacies,* ed. Anderson (see note 20), 11-17; Brian Stanley, *The Bible and the Flag: Protestant Missions and British Imperialism in the Nineteenth and Twentieth Centuries* (Leicester, U.K.: Apollos, 1990), 70-74 and *passim;* and C. C. Ifemesia, "The 'civilising' mission of 1841: aspects of an episode in Anglo-Nigerian relations," in *The History of Christianity in West Africa,* ed. O. U. Kalu (London: Longman, 1980), 81-102.

[24]Latourette, *A History of the Expansion of Christianity, Vol. 5: The Great Century in the Americas, Australia, and Africa* (New York: Harper & Row, 1943), 436; Tim Jeal, *Livingstone* (New York: Putnam, 1973), 41.

on the Christian faith: "THIS alone can penetrate to the root of evil, can teach [the African] to love and to befriend his neighbour, and cause him to act as a candidate for a higher and holier state of being." Buxton continued to rhapsodize, but his rhapsody had a very specific religious anchor: "Let missionaries and schoolmasters, the plough and the spade, go together, and agriculture will flourish; the avenues to legitimate commerce will be opened; confidence between man and man will be inspired; whilst civilization will advance as the natural effect, and Christianity operate as the proximate cause of this happy change."[25]

What makes Buxton relevant for later history is that the triangle of forces he identified as critically important in the 1830s and 1840s have re-emerged in the contemporary world as the critical elements of globalization, whether understood economically, politically or religiously. In our day, evangelical Protestantism joins Roman Catholicism and Islam as the major global religions, modern electronic communications are creating global cultures, and economic exchange that respects no borders defines what globalization means for most ordinary people. Buxton may have been romantic in his own aspirations. Yet his attention to commerce, civilization, and Christianity—and particularly his insistence that trade without Christianity will never produce "a higher and holier state of being"—represents for all Christians a challenge of extraordinary contemporary relevance.

If Christian believers in the twenty-first century offer a religion of hope for the whole world, they will do so not only by rethinking and re-evaluating, but also by revisiting the Niger Valley with Thomas Fowell Buxton. His tying together of economics and Christianity anticipated the tie-in that has developed everywhere today between new life in Christ and new challenges in economic life. In addition, Buxton's notion of "civilization" involved what are now more often seen as concerns of culture. Human beings live within the webs of culture—assumptions about personal relationships, preverbal understandings of what is important and what is not, habits of communication, attitudes toward material goods, toward time, and toward self and others. The

---

[25]Thomas Fowell Buxton, *The African Slave Trade and Its Remedy* (1840; reprint, London: Frank Cass, 1967), 511.

Christian gospel can deeply affect culture, but it never acts independently of what in a particular society is culturally given.

For the communication of the gospel message into the extraordinary diversity of human cultures, no practice has been more powerful than the work of translation. In the introduction to this book we considered in general the effects of translation. Now one last incident sketches some of what went on when evangelicals began to translate the Bible into Korean.

Christian contact with Korea occurred as early as the sixteenth century. It was not, however, until the late eighteenth century that Catholic missionaries were able to bring a sustained Christian witness to this Asian peninsula. Although Catholic converts were persecuted mercilessly, the fortitude of converts and missionaries, supported by some Christian influence seeping in from China and then Japan, sustained a Christian presence in Korea throughout the first three-fourths of the nineteenth century. The modern phase of Christian expansion in Korea began in 1876 when Japan pulled Korea out of its historic dependency upon China and into its own expanding imperial dominance. After the Japanese imposed a law guaranteeing religious freedom, and Korea in 1882 signed a treaty with the United States, Protestant missionaries from Canada, Australia and the United States soon arrived. From the 1880s, Christianity expanded rapidly until at the present about two-fifths of the South Korean population identifies with Christian churches, with Protestants of one sort or another accounting for about four-fifths of that total.[26]

Humanly considered, the rapid advance of Protestantism in Korea came about because of structural factors as well as the religious zeal that many Koreans displayed in practicing their Christian faith. From the first, the indigenizing principles of John Nevius, who visited Korea in 1890, provided the standard for Protestant missionary efforts. Nevius was a veteran missionary to China (from the United States) who shared with Henry Venn of the Church Missionary Society a strong commitment to principles of self-support, self-government and self-propaga-

---

[26]For current figures, see Georg Evers, "Asia," in *The Encyclopedia of Christianity, Vol. 1* (Grand Rapids: Eerdmans, 1999), 137.

tion. With their emphasis on small-group Bible study, the spiritual self-discipline of converts and the missionary as itinerant facilitator, the Nevius principles formalized for mission purposes what was, in effect, the general shape of early Methodist practices in Britain and North America.

Perhaps even more importantly, Protestants entered Korea during a period of manifest social and political crisis. From a long period of domination by China, Korea was being pulled violently into the Japanese orbit. Many historians of Korea have, thus, described Christianity as a religion offering a powerful message of hope for a desperately beleaguered people at an especially critical time.

Also factoring into the rapid Christian expansion, however, was a critical decision with respect to Bible translation. This decision was representative of the kind of Christian-cultural interaction that occurred almost everywhere in the world where Western evangelical missionaries went over the course of the long nineteenth century.[27] And it illustrates what has happened in ever more places, with even broader effects, since the nineteenth century.

Portions of the Scriptures were available in Korean from the late 1700s through the work of Catholic translators working out of China. Protracted debates took place among Catholics over the best Chinese word to use when translating the biblical "God" (this famous "term question" embroiled Catholic officials in Rome and the Far East for a very long time). Eventually, Catholic missionaries working in China at the end of the eighteenth century followed papal instruction by using the Chinese word *T'ien-Chu*. When Catholic translators adapted this Chinese usage for Korea, they transliterated the Chinese word into the Korean *Ch'onju*. Later, however, when the Protestant missionaries arrived, they agreed upon a missionary strategy (finalized at a meeting in

---

[27]My attention was drawn to this subject by a student paper from Sang Hun Roh in fall 1997. The following paragraphs rely upon Sek-Keun O, "Der Volksglaube und das Christentum in Korea" (Ph.D. diss., Free University of Berlin, 1979/Munich: Arbeitsgemeinschaft für Religions- und Weltanschauungsfragen, 1979); Jeong Man Choi, "Historical Development of the Indigenization Movement in the Korean Protestant Church: With Special Reference to Bible Translation" (D.Miss. diss., Fuller Theological Seminary, 1985); Ki Jong So, "The Translation of the Bible into Korean: Its History and Significance" (Ph.D. diss., Drew University, 1993); and the wise personal counsel of Professor Steven Soo-Chan Kang.

1893) directed at the ordinary people, many of whom did not read the formal Korean language that closely followed Chinese. A critical part of this strategy was to undertake a Bible translation that used ordinary Korean (the Hangul) rather than a Chinese-based language. This determination led to the translation of "God" into Korean as *Hananim*, a word that was associated in time-honored Korean history with a more personal deity. Popular Korean resonance with the word *Hananim* was one of the reasons for the appeal of Christianity in Protestant dress.

The use of an indigenous Korean word instead of a borrowed Chinese term for God could, thus, be seen as a noteworthy instance of the indigenous incarnation of the gospel that has been described by Lamin Sanneh.[28] A 1979 dissertation by Sek-Keun O raises the possibility, however, that this indigenization might have been more effective than anyone at the time realized. O suggests that Koreans were comfortable with the word *Hananim* for "God" because it was a word prominent in Korea's historic shamanistic religion—or, to put it more accurately, the shamanistic shape that Confucianism, Buddhism and a number of animistic religions had assumed in Korea. In his interpretation, shamanism is a form of religious practice where the shaman functions as a mediating adept who by contact with the *Hananim* offers multiple services to ordinary believers. Those services include priestly mediation with the divine, healing of bodily ills and prophetic interpretation of events. O argues that shamanistic associations with the worship of *Hananim* reappeared in Korea with a vengeance after the end of Japanese occupation in 1945 and the traumas of migration necessitated by the Korean War. In his interpretation, these events effectively removed the control of external influences (both Japanese and American) and allowed Korean religion to develop along Korean lines. O suggests that an obvious effect of this development was the emergence of syncretistic religions like Sun-Myung Moon's Unification Church, which he characterizes as "a mixture of Christianity with oriental religions, Confucianism, Taoism, Buddhism, and above all shamanism." At the same time, O thinks that more orthodox Protestant groups also displayed

---

[28]See the discussion, with references to Sanneh's work, on pp. 23-25.

"shamanistic peculiarities."[29] He bases this conclusion on the radically fragmenting character of post-War Korean Protestantism, where dozens, if not hundreds, of individual Protestant denominations have been created out of the relative handful of bodies that existed before 1945. As O describes the Korean situation, when leaders of Protestant denominations treat themselves as extraordinary channels of divine revelation, special instruments of divine healing and uniquely inspired interpreters of Scripture, they are acting like Christian shamans.

If O is correct, use of the term *Hananim* made it easier for Koreans to accept the Protestant Christianity that missionaries considered a traditionally Western faith. At the same time, that very translation usage may also have made it easier for the habits of traditional Korean shamanism to be incorporated within the new framework of Protestant Christianity. The process of indigenizing Protestant Christianity in Korea, in other words, may have meant both more and less than the missionaries anticipated: more, because it preserved within the new Christian faith elements of Korean culture that the missionaries thought had been discarded; less, because a successfully transplanted Christianity that moved rapidly to maturity did not necessarily lead to forms of the faith that missionaries recognized as Christian maturity.

*   *   *

In the historical big picture, the nineteenth century witnessed Western evangelical movements expanding out to the world at large. That opening broadened and refined what it meant to be an evangelical. It provided the opportunity to contrast God's power, which redeemed, with human power, which merely called attention to itself. It transformed evangelical culture from a fairly narrow range of Western European, British and North American forms into a bewildering variety of associations with local societies on every continent in the world. The nineteenth century was "great" for evangelicals because it fulfilled the aspiration of John Wesley who claimed the whole world for his parish. It was equally "great" because of the challenges it posed. During the nineteenth century, evangelical Christianity—a renewed old

---

[29]O, "Volksglaube," 212, 201.

religion—was carried around the world. In the twentieth century that religion was planted in even more corners of the globe. In the twenty-first century, evangelical identity will depend in no small part on how evangelical movements put power to use in cultural settings both old and new.

For modern issues of Christian identity, power and culture, few questions are more pertinent than the role the United States and American believers played. Especially for evangelicals, the United States has been a center of activity, programs, personnel and influence spilling out into the world at large. Having traced the situation of Christianity in the world today and sketched a few important events from the nineteenth century, we are now in position to probe how American experience of the Christian faith relates to world Christianity as it has developed over the last one hundred years.

Posing the Question

WHAT, IN FACT, HAS BEEN THE AMERICAN ROLE IN CREATING the new shape of world Christianity and what is now the relation of American Christianity to world Christianity? These important questions are often answered in one of three ways.

First is to assume that Americans control events. For some observers, this control is the same as malevolent manipulation. So understood, religion emanating from the United States has been one additional means—alongside military might and economic self-interest—to capture the world for American interests. A variation of this view, but with the opposite moral evaluation, holds that Americans have indeed shaped the world in their image, but that, at least when it comes to the Christian faith, this shaping has been a good thing. American missionaries, American financial support, American agencies and American influence have, in this picture, been forces for good in transforming the world for Christ. The common point in these contrasting interpretations is to view American action and world reaction as the key matters for the recent history of Christianity. The world, at least to a considerable extent, really is America writ large.

② A second view is to affirm that a strong relationship does exist between Christianity in the United States and Christianity around the world, but also that this relationship is defined much more loosely than simply active American cause and passive global effect. So understood, "influence" rather than "manipulation" becomes the best way for talking about the role of the United States in the world, even as "voluntary choosing" rather than "passive acceptance" is the best way for describing how the rest of the world relates to the United States.

③ A third position sees an even less-direct relationship. It recognizes that newer expressions of Christianity around the world, despite many differences with each other, often do share many characteristics of Christianity in the United States. But in this view, the reason for those similarities is not direct American manipulation, and often not even conscious American influence. Rather, the reason is shared historical experience. Thus, the things that often characterize many of the newer Christian regions in the world look similar to features of American Christianity because they have emerged out of historical circumstances that parallel what Christianity in the United States passed through in its own history. Correlation, not causality, is the key.

Some combination of the second and third positions offers, in my opinion, the best understanding of the American factor in the recent world history of Christianity. In the rest of the book, I try to explain my reasons for that conclusion and for thinking that the first option, which features a concentration on American power—as either a positive or a negative force—is not a particularly useful way to describe what has actually happened.

A SPECIFIC INSTANCE

It might be helpful to provide a concrete example in order to illustrate how these different viewpoints could interpret the same phenomenon. For that purpose, there are few better candidates than the story of a Christian film made in America that has enjoyed a remarkable worldwide distribution. How observers regard its creation and use highlights major differences in interpreting recent world history.

On the night of Saturday, August 19, 2000, at the Roman Catholic

World Youth Day in Rome, and after an address by Pope John Paul II, over one million young people from many countries together watched this particular movie. It was the *Jesus Film*, which had been first produced in 1979 and then aggressively distributed around the world by Campus Crusade for Christ International, the American evangelical parachurch youth ministry founded in 1951. During the four days before August 19, nearly 700,000 videocassettes of the film were distributed to the young people in Rome.[1] The movie is a minimalist presentation of the life of Christ, taken from the Gospel of Luke. It concludes with a direct appeal for viewers to recognize that Jesus, "the Son of God, the Savior, . . . wants to come into your life," and offers a model prayer that includes the statement, "I open the door of my life and receive you as Savior and Lord."[2]

Ten weeks before the mass viewing of this movie in Rome, and halfway around the world in Chandigarh, Punjab state, India, Mr. Ashish Prabhash was first stabbed and then burned in his home, possibly by right-wing Hindu militants. The murdered man worked for India Campus Crusade for Christ and was engaged in showing the *Jesus Film* to rural villagers in his region.[3] Six years earlier four Rwandans who also worked with Campus Crusade in showing the film had been among the many victims in that nation's tragic genocide.[4]

As part of its strategy for using this movie, Campus Crusade has undertaken mass distribution of the *Jesus Film* in the United States, with the postal service in the year 2000 delivering video copies to 1.1 million homes in ten U.S. cities (at a cost of approximately $3 million) and then in even larger quantities the next year, including a distribution to 7 million homes in Texas, where the *Houston Chronicle* reported that the movie was put to especially good use by the Rev. Khanh Huynh, pastor of a Vietnamese Baptist Church in Houston, and the Rev. John

---

[1]Paul A. Eshleman, "The 'Jesus' Film: A Contribution to World Evangelism," *International Bulletin of Missionary Research* 26 (April 2002): 68.

[2]Inspirational Films/The Genesis Project, *Jesus* (1979; Liguna Niguel, Calif.: Campus Crusade for Christ).

[3]Asia Intelligence Wire, *Financial Times*, *The Hindu*, June 12 and June 17, 2000. All references to the *Jesus Film* from local newspapers were downloaded from Lexis-Nexis on February 16, 2002. I thank Ethan Schrum for doing this work.

[4]*St. Petersburg Times*, August 6, 1994, 4.

Sanchez, director of Hispanic outreach for the College of Biblical Studies.[5] Extensive as these U.S. efforts were, Campus Crusade has been doing even more to get the *Jesus Film* into circulation outside the United States. During 2000, for example, videocassettes were distributed to 200,000 homes in Leicester, Carlisle and the London borough of Lewisham, in the United Kingdom; plans were set in motion to deliver it to every household in Invercargill, New Zealand, one of the southernmost cities on the planet; and Campus Crusade released a DVD of the film that could be viewed with eight separate languages—Arabic, English, French, Japanese, Korean, Mandarin Chinese, Portuguese and Spanish—thus providing a version understandable to over half the people in the world.[6]

The phenomenal scale of distribution for the *Jesus Film,* which we will examine further in a later chapter, suggests a number of important features concerning the American evangelical contribution to the recent world history of Christianity.

- The Campus Crusade film is representative of the globalization of trade, goods and culture—as well as religion—in which the United States has played a leading part.

- It speaks of the large number of American volunteers who have left their own shores to work as missionaries in other lands and of the relatively ample funding that has supported them.

- The film also illustrates a characteristically American alliance of advanced technology and evangelistic zeal.

- Most importantly, it displays the conversionistic and voluntaristic character of much American religion—that is, the stress on an active individual choice for Christ (conversion) and an active personal initiative in promoting Christianity (voluntarism).

- In addition, as illustrated by the case of Ashish Prabhash, the film

---

[5]On the 2000 distribution, *Los Angeles Times*, Dec. 6, 2000, Metro-B, 4; *Seattle Times*, Dec. 9, 2000, A11; *Atlanta Constitution*, Dec. 16, 2000, F; and on the Texas distribution, *The Houston Chronicle*, Religion, March 17, 2001, 1.

[6]*Leicester Mercury*, Nov. 22, 1999, 13; *Southland Times* (N.Z.), June 5, 1999, 30; *Christianity Today*, Dec. 6, 1999, 22 (the DVD).

shows the cultural disruption caused in some places where Americans have carried their conversionist, voluntaristic understanding of the Christian gospel.

But now the questions of interpretation: What does the *Jesus Film* represent as an illustration of United States connections to the world? First, it is possible to view the film and its use as a straightforward American attempt to exert religious control over the world. If you like the message of the film, you might see its distribution as heroic; if you think its distribution ruins local cultures, you might consider it destructive. The common point of interpretation, however, would stress the American angles: American funding that made possible this American missionary tool; American management that organized distribution of the film; the willingness of others to promote the film as an instance of American control; their acceptance or rejection of the film's message as acceptance or rejection of the United States. In this picture, the way that the film has shaped religious life to whatever degree in whichever corner of the globe testifies to the ongoing weight of an American presence in local religious life.

Alternatively, the second interpretation would note the very same American actions in creating and distributing the film, but would see a great deal of local initiative or agency accompanying the initiative of Americans. ("Agency" here means the exercise of control or power.) Thus, American provision of the film for showing in India or Rwanda does speak to genuine influence from the United States, but the willingness of local Christian believers to sign up as agents for the film's distribution speaks also of meaningful choices made in locations far from the United States for purposes that may have very little to do with what Americans want or don't want. Likewise, accepting or rejecting the message of the film may not concern primarily a response to American influence, but rather an action keyed to the viewers' own responses for the viewers' own reasons.

The third interpretation acknowledges much from the others: Yes, American influence is unquestioned, but, yes also, local peoples are not mere automatons in choosing to use American-provided materials for their own religious purposes. But it goes on to ask why the film can now be used widely as it is being used, and why it has had the extensive effects it is now having. The film depicts the key to Christian faith as a personal choice for Jesus Christ, followed by a life of dedicated personal service guided by Christian norms and oriented toward Christian goals. Its depiction of Christianity does not emphasize church structures or sacraments, historic Christian institutions, authority exercised by established church officials, or the traditional debates among Christians that have been so much a part of Western Christian history. The film's message is thus quite similar to one that resonated with special strength in the earlier history of the United States, when rapidly growing populations in unsettled, often frontier conditions turned to Christianity for both personal salvation from sin and guidance for creating orderly communities out of social and cultural chaos.

In this interpretation, the conversionistic and voluntaristic message of the *Jesus Film* offers both personal hope and guidance for cultural security among peoples who are experiencing unsettled, disorienting social circumstances. In other words, the *Jesus Film* illustrates not just American influence and not just local agency in responding to (or rejecting) the film but also a type of Christian appeal matched to contemporary circumstances. In turn, this appeal is similar to the type of Christian appeal that became so formative in the United States during a period when it was marked by social and cultural developments that paralleled what many societies are experiencing in the world today.

These three interpretations of the *Jesus Film* are not mutually exclusive. They do, however, lead to quite different conclusions about the American factor in the recent development of Christianity around the world.

WHY THE QUESTION MATTERS

Why does the question of the United States' relation to the rest of world Christianity matter? The answers to that question are mostly self-evident, though it is good to try to spell them out.

Most obviously, the United States is today the world's richest nation and also the strongest military power in the world. General reactions to American power of course vary tremendously given different circumstances. On the United States' military might, for example, in the late 1980s there was considerable favorable world opinion about the role of American military pressure in ending communist rule in Eastern Europe and the former Soviet Union. In the immediate aftermath of the terrorist attacks of September 2001, there was much world sympathy for the U.S.-led invasion of Afghanistan. From 2003 there has been much scorn for the United States' invasion of Iraq. It is much the same for the U.S. economy. Over the last two decades, increasing respect and reliance (some of it grudging) has come from China, India and other developing countries as they join the ranks of developed nations who have long benefited from trade and financial ties with the United States. Over the same decades, increasingly vocal complaints have also been voiced about the United States' role in distorting local economies, manipulating national financial prospects, and refusing to acknowledge the very large American contribution to global warming. To the extent, therefore, that Christian influences from the United States are linked to the United States' economic and military activity, these activities become part of the American factor in world Christianity.

It is the same for the United States' role as the world's largest exporter of popular cultural styles in technology, music and movies. For better and for worse, American leadership in these spheres can easily be linked to the perceived Christian character of the United States. Radical Muslims complain bitterly about the damage that so-called Christian America is doing to the world, and some of that complaint is easily recognized as sheer demagoguery. But not all. Steven Keillor is one evangelical who believes that some aspects of the Islamicist indictment of the United States should be taken seriously. At the end of a thoughtful argument about whether to consider the terrorist attacks of 2001 as a divine judgment on the U.S., Keillor draws this conclusion: "We arrive at this cautious, cause-restricted interpretation of September 11 as possibly God's judgment on us for our materialism, our cultural exports seducing others into immorality, and our use of terroristic guerilla units against the Soviets [in Afghanistan]."[7]

---

[7]Steven J. Keillor, *God's Judgments: Interpreting History and the Christian Faith* (Downers Grove, Ill.: InterVarsity Press, 2007), 59.

This conclusion merits sober reflection, but much else is involved in American leadership of technology, popular culture, economics and the military. Use of the internet for all manner of purposes—some unquestionably evil, some almost as unquestionably good—points to the complexity of judging these aspects of the American factor in world Christianity. Equally complex must be judgments about the United States' global economic influence—on the one side, it can promote greed, inequality and exploitation; on the other, it can open opportunities, create jobs and alleviate poverty.

Beyond the realms of geopolitics, economics and popular culture, the place of the United States in the world's church history, narrowly considered, also highlights the significance of the American factor. For Roman Catholicism, the United States is vitally important for a number of reasons. The mostly positive experience of Catholics with American democracy played an important role at the Second Vatican Council when the church as a whole followed the guidance of American theologians in affirming the foundational importance of religious liberty. American Catholics also contribute a disproportionately large share of the total financial resources for their church. American volunteers make up a significant number of the church's workers employed full time for social justice. Within the United States itself, the Catholic Church represents perhaps the most multi-ethnic organization of any kind, and so is a major laboratory for crosscultural cooperation and crosscultural communication completely within the nation's borders.

For Eastern Orthodox Christians, the United States is the most important region in the world where national conditions do not reinforce the division of Orthodoxy into ethnic enclaves and where its ethnic members are sometimes mixed. In particular, the Orthodox Church in America (OCA), an offshoot of the Russian Orthodox Church, and the Antiochean Orthodox Church have been leaders in seeking fellowship among the various Orthodox communions, planting new churches that use English as the worshiping language, and receiving converts from other Christian movements. In a world where Orthodoxy suffered massive pressure from Communist regimes throughout the twentieth century, the United Sates may be the place where Orthodoxy has the greatest chance to break free from its narrowly ethnic traditions. If that effacement of ethnicity for Orthodoxy will happen anywhere in the world, it is most likely to occur in the United States.

The history of Protestants in the United States brings us closer to the main themes of this book. From early in its history, the United States was the prime promoter of religion practiced on the basis of disestablishment, or the independence of churches from the state and vice versa. During the seventeenth and eighteenth centuries, some religious tolerance could be found in Britain and Holland for upstart religious groups not connected to established state-supported churches. Yet the idea that Christian believers in large numbers could form effective churches without formal state authority was a radically new idea in the United States. Indeed, from its beginning, the chance to live under such a system had been a primary motive for some who came to this New World. Yet far back into European Christian history, another pattern was axiomatic; it was almost universally believed that if Christianity was true, it deserved support from government, even as church institutions provided governments and public institutions their benediction and support.

In the United States things worked out differently. At first for mostly pragmatic reasons and in regions (like the middle colonies) where no single church dominated, various religious groups learned to get along without any one of them enjoying state-church privileges. By the late eighteenth century, what had begun as pragmatic practice became a principle: leaders concerned about public good and leaders concerned about the health of the churches agreed that the separation of church and state would be best for all. Eventually, even Christian traditions that had defended establishment in Europe as a sine qua non for true religion came to accept this American way for carrying out their religious organization, activity and financing. Thus it was that Catholics, Lutherans, Presbyterians and Episcopalians, who had almost always contended for official recognition and official support in Europe, became in the United States willing advocates of a "free church" pattern of religious life.

The significance for world Christianity of this momentous shift should be obvious. While many of the world's Muslim leaders and a few of its Christians continue to defend the principle of interlocking religious, social, legal and educational institutions, most of the world has moved or is moving rapidly beyond what had once been an almost universal practice. As they do so, the nation that pioneered such a step takes on additional significance.

The church history of the United States is also of worldwide significance for its role in the origins and spread of Pentecostalism. As we will see in chapter seven, it is no longer possible to think about the story of Pentecostalism as beginning at one solitary American place and at only one point in time (Los Angeles' Azusa Street mission in 1906). Yet the events at Azusa Street in 1906—when great numbers responded to William Seymour's preaching that advocated the baptism of the Holy Spirit—did reverberate far and wide. The general enthusiasm found at Azusa Street for divine healing, speaking and praying in tongues, and special words of prophecy given by God was soon communicated to many corners of the globe. If today as much as one-fourth of all Christian adherents in the world are in some sense Pentecostal, it means that questions about the emergence of the Pentecostal emphases are important questions for contemporary life as well as historical curiosity. Whether the Pentecostal manifestations so widespread in the world today sustain a genetic connection to Azusa Street or flourish in circumstances in some way resembling the situation at Azusa Street, the American factor remains an important question.

* * *

In sum, general consideration of Christianity in the world today demands a recognition of the fact that the United States is a great world power. Yet even more important than American power is the nation's particular church history and the history of American Christianity developed by interaction with the broader American society. In turn, if the relationship between American Christianity and world Christianity involves parallel historical development more than direct influence, then efforts to assess the quality of Christian life in America become more important than attempts simply to assess the nature and extent of American influence.

What Does Counting
Missionaries Reveal?

ONE APPROACH TO ASSESSING THE AMERICAN FACTOR IN contemporary world Christianity is to focus on the number, origin and character of missionaries. In fact, however, a complete investigation would require an interpretation of the role missionaries play in the expansion of Christianity. For that purpose, the best scholarship increasingly describes missionary activity as a necessary, but not sufficient, explanation for the emergence of new Christian churches. The best regular presentation of that scholarship comes in the pages of the *International Bulletin of Missionary Research*, the premier journal for world Christian concerns, and through books from Orbis Press, which for several decades has led American publishers in serious consideration of newer forms of world Christianity. This high-quality work on Christian expansion almost always documents a combination of missionary beginnings and indigenous development. With only a few exceptions, missionaries regularly provided the beginning points that have led to full-scale church development in the world's new Christian regions.

After those beginning points, missionary contributions have varied widely—sometimes providing guidance and support to new Christian churches for generations, sometimes fading away rapidly after the initial impetus. But in the accounts with the best research and the most convincing narratives, a common pattern appears relatively early in the description of development. That pattern involves local appropriation of Christianity by local agents for local reasons and in the context of local cultural realities.

Examples of that process now abound in the best research on Christianity in the contemporary world. So, as examples, in writing about the twentieth-century explosion of Christianity in Africa, Adrian Hastings, Paul Kollman and Diane Stinton have all underscored the importance of a wide variety of missionary efforts, but all have also painstakingly documented the common process by which "missionary Christianity" sooner or later became "African Christianity."[1] Susan Billington Harper's masterful portrait of V. S. Azariah, the first Anglican bishop in India, describes a large-scale debt to the YMCA and various British missions, but also the eventual emergence of a Christian witness much more obviously Indian than colonial.[2] The same pattern appears in Ryan Dunch's account of Christian development in China during the first half of the twentieth century—missionary activity followed by indigenous Chinese direction of indigenous Chinese churches.[3] It is the same in the Pacific Islands where, as documented by Ian Breward, several generations of Catholic and Protestant missionaries have led on to several generations of multiform Pacific Island Christianity.[4] It is likewise similar for Latin America, where Paul Freston and his colleagues have noted extensive missionary activity, but convinc-

---

[1]Adrian Hastings, *The Church in Africa, 1450-1950* (New York: Oxford University Press, 1994); Paul V. Kollman, *The Evangelization of Slaves and Catholic Origins in Eastern Africa* (Maryknoll, N.Y.: Orbis, 2005); Diane B. Stinton, *Jesus of Africa: Voices of Contemporary African Christology* (Maryknoll, N.Y.: Orbis, 2004).
[2]Susan Billington Harper, *In the Shadow of the Mahatma: Bishop V. S. Azariah and the Travails of Christianity in British India* (Grand Rapids: Eerdmans, 2000).
[3]Ryan Dunch, *Fuzhou Protestants and the Making of a Modern China* (New Haven: Yale University Press, 2001).
[4]Ian Breward, *A History of the Churches in Australasia* (New York: Oxford University Press, 2001).

ingly demonstrate the leadership of Latin American churches by Latin Americans.[5] And in the key works on world Pentecostalism by David Martin and Allan Anderson, missionary activity is rapidly eclipsed by the self-directed movement toward Pentecostal expression in Latin America, Africa, Korea and other regions.[6]

When, therefore, we focus on the numbers and character of the American missionary force, we are examining one aspect of an important part of the recent world history of Christianity. But it is no more than that. Other accounts must fill in what an examination of American missionary personnel cannot supply, which is the full story of how Christian proclamation leads on to church development and then, in turn, to the active presence of solidly rooted Christian movements. Nonetheless, even an overview of world missionary service over the last century does reveal a great deal about the American factor in world Christianity.

MISSIONARY NUMBERS

Such an examination is particularly helpful as one way to assess America's role in the world and the effect of American Christianity on world Christianity. To be sure, counting missionaries, except among well-organized hierarchical bodies like the Roman Catholic Church or the Church of Jesus Christ of Latter-day Saints (Mormons), is always a risky venture, at best. But since about 1900, international organizations and several American agencies have tried to provide reliable information on the numbers, funding and location of Christian missionaries. Despite problems of precision, a digest of that information, as summarized in tables 5.1 and 5.2, points toward at least a few conclusions.

As tables 5.1 and 5.2 indicate, the American proportion of the worldwide Protestant missionary force rose rapidly at the start of the twentieth century, continued to grow until reaching about two-thirds of the world total in the early 1970s, and still continues at a high proportion

---

[5]Paul Freston, ed., *Evangelical Christianity and Democracy in Latin America* (New York: Oxford University Press, 2008).

[6]David Martin, *Pentecostalism: The World Their Parish* (Oxford: Blackwell, 2002); Allan Anderson, *An Introduction to Pentecostalism: Global Charismatic Christianity* (New York: Cambridge University Press, 2004).

Table 5.1

Overseas Missionary Personnel (World and United States)

	Total Prot. Missionaries	U.S. Protestants	U.S. % of total	U.S. R.C.	U.S. Mormons
1903	15,288	ca. 4,000	26%		
1911	20,333	ca. 7,900	39%		
1925	29,188				
1932				866	
1935		11,899			
1952		12,536			
1960		ca. 27,400			
1963				7,000	
1968		ca. 33,000		9,655	
1970				8,373	
1972	ca. 52,500	34,057	65%	7,691	13,000
1979		50,691		6,455	
1985		64,789		6,056	27,000
1991				5,595	
1999		41,702+100,752		5,854	
2001	97,732	46,381	47%		

N.B. Until the 1990s, efforts to count usually combined long-term missionaries (career or more than one year) and short-term missionaries (less than one year). The Protestant numbers for 1999 offer the number of long-term missionaries and then the number of short-term (less than one year) missionaries. The numbers for 2001 are for long-term, career missionaries. Most Mormon missionaries are two-year appointees.

Sources: (total Protestants 1903, 1991, 1925) Harlan P. Beach and Charles H. Fahs, *World Missionary Atlas* (New York: Institute of Social and Religious Research, 1925), 76. (U.S. Protestants 1903, 1911) Charles W. Forman, "The Americas," *International Bulletin of Missionary Research* 6 (Apr. 1982): 54. (Roman Catholics) "Missions, Catholic (U.S.)," *New Catholic Encyclopedia, vol. XVII: Supplement: Change in the Church* (New York: McGraw-Hill, 1979), 428-29; *Mission Handbook 1991-1992* (Washington: U.S. Catholic Mission Association, 1992), 28-29; Matthew Bunson, ed., *Catholic Almanac 2002* (Huntingdon, Ind.: Our Sunday Visitor, 2002), 447-48. (Protestants 1935, 1952) Joel A. Carpenter, "Appendix: The Evangelical Missionary Force in the 1930s," in *Earthen Vessels: American Evangelicals and Foreign Missions, 1880-1980*, ed. Carpenter and Wilbert R. Shenk (Grand Rapids: Eerdmans, 1990), 335-42. (1972) Edward R. Dayton, ed., *Mission Handbook 1973* (Monrovia, Calif.: MARC, 1973). (1979, 1985) Samuel Wilson and John Siewert, eds., *Mission Handbook*, 13th ed. (Monrovia, Calif.: MARC, 1986); (1999) A. Scott Moreau, "Putting the Survey in Perspective," in *Mission Handbook 2001-2003*, ed. John A Siewert and Dotsey Wellner, 18th ed. (Wheaton, Ill.: EMIS, 2001), 33-79. (2001) Patrick Johnstone and Jason Mandryk, *Operation World* (Carlisle, U.K.: Paternoster, 2001), 747. Note: The *Mission Handbook, 2007-2009*, ed. Linda J. Weber and Dotsey Welliver (Wheaton, Ill.: EMIS, 2007), is an excellent resource, but the way mission agencies reported data makes it somewhat difficult to compare with earlier years.

Table 5.2

Number of U.S. Agencies Founded

1900s	16
1910s	23
1920s	22
1930s	34
1940s	55
1950s	70
1960s	81
1970s	123
1980s	141
1990-1998	66

Source: *Mission Handbook 2001-2003*, 36.

Table 5.3

Missionary Force 1972: U.S. Protestant, U.S. Roman Catholic, British Protestant

	U.S. Protestant	*U.S. R.C.*	*British Protestant*
Africa	7,671	1,107	2,268
Asia	8,700	2,014	1,566
Europe & USSR	1,871	39	648
Latin America	9,592	3,429	648
Oceania	860	826	270
Total	29,290	7,415	5,400

Source: *Mission Handbook 1973*, 84.

despite the recent surge in Protestant missionary volunteers from other countries. That surge is significant for the larger purposes of this paper, however, for it suggests that the number of Protestant missionary volunteers not from the United States has been increasing much more rapidly than the number of American volunteers. Table 5.2, which shows the rate at which new Protestant missionary agencies were created in the United States, indicates steady growth throughout the century, and then a special acceleration in the four decades after World War II. Only in the 1990s did the pace of forming new missionary organizations slacken somewhat.

Table 5.3, which presents comparative information for overseas missionary personal for the year 1972, illustrates the world situation in greater detail. Britain, which at the start of the century had sent out the most Protestant missionaries, now trailed the United States by a factor of five. The number of American Roman Catholic personnel serving overseas was also larger than the British Protestant force. This same table also reveals the leadership of Protestants in American missionary ventures, since in the early 1970s the ratio of Protestant to Catholic missionaries was almost 4 to 1, while the ratio of self-identified Protestants to Catholics in the United States as a whole was only about 2.4 to 1.[7] Even considering the difficulties of precise enumeration, it is clear that American missionaries, especially American Protestant missionaries, had grown significantly by comparison to the missionary efforts of other Protestant countries.

EVANGELICALS AMONG AMERICAN MISSIONARIES

The next tables provide information pointing indirectly to broader developments in the world. Within the American Protestant missionary force, the number of evangelicals rose steadily throughout the century from a substantial minority to, at present, an overwhelming majority. In general terms, major American religious groupings reveal this general pattern throughout the century. Catholic missionary work began only in the early years of the century, rose steadily in number of participants until the late 1960s, and then has declined gradually since that time. Missionary activity of the mainline Protestant denominations dominated American missionary efforts at the start of the century, remained strong into the 1950s, and then trailed off significantly since that time. By contrast, evangelical (and Mormon) missionaries made up only a minority of Protestant missionaries early in the century but have continued to expand until they now constitute all but a small fraction of American missionary efforts.

---

[7]The Gallup Poll in 1971 indicated that 65 percent of Americans identified themselves as Protestants and 26 percent as Catholics (2.5:1). For 1974, the same poll resulted in self-description results of 60 percent Protestant and 27 percent Catholic (2.2:1). *Religion in America, 1977-78*, The Gallup Opinion Index no. 145 (Princeton: American Institute of Public Opinion, 1978), 37.

Table 5.4

U.S. Protestant Missionaries Serving Overseas

(A) MAINLINE PROTESTANT DENOMINATIONS

	1935–36	1952	1972	1999
Presbyterian Church (USA)*	2,100	1,805	1,005	772
United Methodist*	1,388	1,667	951	413
ABFMS	495	354	262	120+3
United Church of Canada	452		210	96
Protestant Episcopal	427	207	198	21+32
United Christian Missionary Society	173	213	673	??
United Church of Christ			244	126

ABFMS = American Baptist Foreign Mission Society

*Methodist and Presbyterian totals for earlier years include numbers from denominations that later merged into the larger continuing denominations.

(B) EVANGELICAL DENOMINATIONS

	1935–36	1952	1972	1999
Southern Baptists (1845)	405	855	2,507	4,562
Churches of Christ			1,623	2,168
Assemblies of God (1914)	230	626	967	1,543
Baptist Bible Fellowship (1950)			379	755
Christian & Missionary Alliance (1887)	447	667	803	726
Ass. Baptists for World Evangel. (1927)			351	716
Baptist Mid Missions (1920)			511	612
Evangelical Free Church (1887)	32	101	181	ca. 600
Mission to the World—PCA				579
CBInternational (1943)				550
Church of the Nazarene (1908)	88	200	495	487
Seventh-day Adventists	1,240	1,107	1,546	514
Mennonite Board (1920)	52	109	454	200
(Swed.) Evangelical Covenant (1885)	38	123	94	92+15
Free Methodists (1885)	141	102	198	75

PCA = Presbyterian Church in America; CB = Conservative Baptists

(C) INTERDENOMINATIONAL AGENCIES

	1935–36	1952	1972	1999
Wycliffe Bible Translators (1935)			2,200	2,930
YWAM (1961)			1,009	1,817
New Tribes Mission (1942)			701	1,514
Campus Crusade for Christ (1951)			114	973
TEAM (1890)	95	636	992	638
SIM (1893)			818	569
Frontiers (1972)				311
Gospel Missionary Union (1892)	42	120	288	163+34
OMF International (1865)			562	156
Operation Mobilization (1957)				171

YWAM = Youth With a Mission; TEAM = The Evangelical Alliance Mission; SIM = Serving in Mission (until the 1980s, Sudan Interior Mission); OMF = Overseas Missionary Fellowship (previously China Inland Mission)

Sources: Carpenter, "Evangelical Missionary Force"; *Mission Handbook 1973*, 89, 97-99; *Mission Handbook 2001-2003*, 51.

Table 5.5

Evangelical Proportion of U.S. Protestant Missionary Force

(A) THROUGHOUT THE TWENTIETH CENTURY

1935	40% (4,784 of 11,899)
1952	49% (6,146 of 12,536)
1999	91% (38,044 of 41,957)

(B) IN 1999

	No. of agencies	Combined budgets
Evangelical	1,019	$2.37 billion
Mainline	84	$0.52 billion
Other	10	$0.04 billion

"Evangelical" includes groups self-identified as independent, fundamentalist, Pentecostal, as well as evangelical.

Sources: Carpenter, "Evangelical Missionary Force"; *Mission Handbook 2001-2003*, 41.

Admittedly, the designations of "evangelical" and "mainline" are fluid. But for the preparation of these tables I have defined as "evangelical" the strongly conversionist groups that stress the characteristics singled out by David Bebbington in his helpful definition (conversion, Bible, the cross of Christ and activism). So defined, the mainline Protestant missionary force would always contain some evangelicals, but would often also stress humanitarian and development programs instead of evangelization. Many of the evangelical groups also do humanitarian and development work, but always alongside of rather than as a replacement for conversion.

One additional trend is obvious from tables 5.4B, 5.4C and 5.6. Especially in the last half of the twentieth century, nondenominational evangelical missionary societies grew much more rapidly than denominational agencies. This development is significant because, in general, the nondenominational agencies tend to be even more aggressively conversionistic than the missionaries from evangelical denominations. In addition, funding for the nondenominational societies is completely entrepreneurial—those who want to be missionaries make contact with

Table 5.6

U.S. Protestant Missionary Agencies

	denominational	*nondenominational*
1900	74%	26%
1940	55%	45%
1960	34%	66%
1980	26%	74%
1998	18%	82%

Source: *Mission Handbook 2001-03*, 39.

their own friends and with individual local churches and from these personal connections gather funds for their own financial support. If leaders of these nondenominational agencies envision large-scale projects (like Campus Crusade's *Jesus Film*), their leaders must secure the money on their own.

The contrast with fundraising among evangelical denominations is not in most cases great, since missionaries affiliated with evangelical denominations usually raise their own financial support in the same way. The major exception is the Southern Baptist Convention, which raises money for its missionaries collectively as a denomination and then as a denomination commissions and funds missionaries for their work. This corporate funding scheme, however, is standard among the missionary programs of the mainline Protestant denominations.

The larger point is to observe that, with the prime exception of the Southern Baptists, the American missionary programs that are most conversionistic in their message are also the most voluntaristic in their methods. Precisely these most conversionistic and voluntaristic mission societies have come to dominate the American missionary force over the course of the last half-century.

Many examples could be offered to illustrate the rapid growth and extensive spread of these evangelical missionary organizations. World Vision, a development and relief agency founded in 1950 to assist orphans in Korea and elsewhere in Asia, during the year 2001 raised $964 million, with about 55 percent coming from American sources. To put that figure into comparative perspective, the income of the World Council of Churches in 1999 was about $27 million (roughly 40 percent from Germany), or only one thirty-fifth of the World Vision total.[8] Another example of a rapid start-up, Youth With a Mission (YWAM), was founded by Loren Cunningham in 1961 as an organization to involve young Americans in spreading Christian faith, meeting human health and nutrition needs, and starting churches. In 2001 YWAM employed nearly twelve thousand workers drawn from all over the world, with only about one-sixth of them from the United States.[9]

In some sense these missionary agencies play out in local settings and mostly out of the public eye what the globetrotting evangelist Billy Graham did in fully public display throughout his long career. Graham, though stationed in the United States and often busy with evangelistic campaigns in American cities, became the John Wesley of his era because he took the whole world for his parish. During the three-year period 1958-1960, for example, Graham preached before large crowds at multiple sites in the Caribbean, Africa, Europe, Australia, New Zealand and the United States; during the three-year period 1988-1990, he did the same at multiple sites in the People's Republic of China, the USSR, Canada, England, Hungary, West Germany, Hong Kong and again the United States. And he had carried on in the same way for most of the intervening thirty years.[10] In this peripatetic evangelization, Graham was certainly an agent for Christ, but he was also a representative of America and an American version of the Christian faith.

Yet for sheer scale and reach, there has been as yet nothing to compare with Campus Crusade's *Jesus Film* project.[11] The founder of Cam-

[8]For World Vision, www.wvi.org/home (accessed March 6, 2002). The World Council of Churches figure was reported on its website as 45.4 million Swiss francs. *Briefing Book on International Organizations in Geneva*, U.S. Mission to the United Nations in Geneva, http://www.genevabriefingbook.com/chapters/wcc.html (accessed March 6, 2002).
[9]For the story of this organization, see Loren Cunningham, *Is That Really You, God?* with "A Word About the Supernatural" from John Sherrill (Grand Rapids: Chosen Books, 1984).
[10]Extensively documented in William Martin, *A Prophet with Honor: The Billy Graham Story* (New York: Morrow, 1991); and Billy Graham, *Just As I Am: The Autobiography of Billy Graham* (New York: HarperSanFrancisco, 1997).
[11]Unless noted otherwise, information is from Paul A. Eshleman, "The 'Jesus' Film: A Contribution to World Evangelism," *International Bulletin of Missionary Research* 26 (April 2002):

pus Crusade, Bill Bright, apparently was thinking about using film for mass evangelism even before he founded the organization in 1951. Bright's thoughts took concrete form when in the mid-1970s he met John Heyman, a Jewish filmmaker, who had established the Genesis Project in order to film all the narratives of the entire Bible. Heyman had completed short films of the first twenty chapters of Genesis and the first two chapters of Luke when he was urged to contact Campus Crusade for help in marketing the films to Christian groups. In 1979 Heyman finished his full-length feature on the life of Christ based on the Gospel of Luke, which was then released for commercial distribution. Two years later Campus Crusade secured distribution rights and began its own effort, which in the words of the project's director was "to show the 'Jesus' film to every person in the world in an understandable language and in a setting near where they live."[12]

As we have already seen, energetic labor by translators and dubbers, a wide network of American and non-American workers, and a steady flow of primarily American donations have combined for a staggering result. The film has been shown in every village of Mongolia with over two hundred fifty people. It has been shown in over four hundred thousand villages of India in fifty-one languages. It is available in eighteen different languages for showing in South Africa. Most of the population of Burundi and 40 percent of the population of Rwanda has seen the film.[13] Mother Teresa asked that the film be shown in all her houses for the dying in Calcutta. It is available for downloading from the internet in fifty-five languages, with Arabic being the most often requested language, after English.

In the aggregate, as of mid-2007, the film was available in 1,005 different languages, with an additional 197 translations under preparation; according to Campus Crusade's statistics, it had been viewed by nearly six billion people in 229 countries; over 43 million videocassettes had been distributed; Campus Crusade was using 4,418 full-time work-

68-72; and The Jesus Film Project official website, www.jesusfilm.org (accessed July 19, 2007).
[12]Eshleman, "'Jesus' Film," 69.
[13]Information on South Africa, Burundi and Rwanda is from Patrick Johnstone and Jason Mandryk, *Operation World* (Carlisle, U.K.: Paternoster, 2001), 136, 552, 582.

ers in 2,143 teams to show the film in 106 different countries; and the film showing can be connected to the start-up of over 100,000 new churches. The most active promoters of the film have been the mission boards of two American evangelical denominations (Southern Baptist Convention, Church of the Nazarene), two American interdenominational agencies (World Vision and Operation Mobilization) and the Roman Catholic Church.

In the face of such a flood of numbers, it is well to heed the cautious reminder well stated by the American religious historian Leigh Schmidt: "Most of the things that count about Christianity cannot be counted, like the warmth or coolness of prayer, the resonance or hollowness of scriptural words, the songs or silences of the saints in heaven, the presences or absences in the sacrament."[14] It is also appropriate to note theological criticism of the film, as from the Lutheran minister, Ronald Marshall, who criticized the movie for removing most of the "hard words" from Luke's gospel, like references to "the powerful" being "put down" in Mary's "Magnificat" from Luke 1.[15]

Even more germane to the concerns of this book, it is important to remember how the American concern for enumerating Christian work can look to non-Americans. Kanzo Uchimura (1861-1930) was a Japanese Christian evangelist and Bible teacher who as a young man studied in the United States and thereafter made many visits to North America. Toward the end of his life in 1926 he wrote at some length about his impressions of Christianity in the United States:

> Americans are great people; there is no doubt about that. They are great in building cities and railroads. . . . Americans have a wonderful genius for improving breeds of horses, cattle, sheep and swine. . . . Americans too are great inventors. . . . Needless to say, they are great in money. . . . Americans are great in all these things and much else; but not in Religion. . . . Americans must count religion in order to see or show its value. . . . To them big churches are successful churches. . . . To win the

---

[14]Leigh E. Schmidt, "Mixed Blessings: Christianization and Secularization," *Reviews in American History* 26 (Dec. 1998): 640.

[15]Ronald F. Marshall, "Debunking the Jesus Video Project," *Lutheran Forum* (Christmas/ Winter 1999): 50-51. The next issue of this orthodox Lutheran publication contained several strenuous defenses of the movie.

greatest number of converts with the least expense is their constant endeavour. Statistics is their way of showing success or failure in their religion as in their commerce and politics. Numbers, numbers, oh, how they value numbers![16]

To Uchimura, the American churches did their work under the guidance of American cultural imperatives. Uchimura elsewhere had many positive things to say about American religious life, but he was struck by how much the norms of an acquisitive, market-driven and aggressively statistical culture had shaped the perspective of the churches. However regarded, American activity like Campus Crusade's *Jesus Film* does show the aggressiveness with which American Protestants—with evangelicals in the lead—have carried their message to other parts of the world.

RESULTS OF MISSIONARY EFFORTS?

But what have been the effects of American missionary service on world Christian developments? More particularly, how important have Americans been in the transformation of world Christianity that has taken place over the last century? That transformation, it is important to remember, has involved a breathtaking series of huge structural changes. To the material on the new situation presented in chapter two, further comparisons are helpful for noting the scale of change. When the great Edinburgh Missionary Conference was held in 1910, over 80 percent of the world's affiliated Christian population lived in Europe and North America. Today, less than 40 percent of the world's Christian population lives in Europe and North America, and Europe's self-professed believers are among the world's least active Christians in terms of church attendance, Bible reading and Christian education.

The 2001 edition of David Barrett's *World Christian Encyclopedia* provides especially significant information about the worldwide sweep

---

[16]Kanzo Uchimura, "Can Americans Teach Japanese Religion?" *Japan Christian Intelligencer* 1 (1926): 357-61, as quoted here from *The Complete Works of Kanzo Uchimura*, 7 vols. (Tokyo: Kyobunkwan, 1972), 4:63-65. I was introduced to Uchimura and his opinions on American religion by Andrew F. Walls, *The Missionary Movement in Christian History* (Maryknoll, N.Y.: Orbis, 1996), 221-22.

of evangelical and evangelical-like movements. Using Barrett's narrow-est definition of "evangelical," the encyclopedia found that more "evan-gelicals" lived in the United States (40.6 million) than anywhere else in the world, but also that the next most populous "evangelical" countries were two where almost no evangelicals had existed one hundred years ago: Brazil (27.7 million) and Nigeria (22.3 million).[17] Of the next four countries where Barrett found the largest number of evangelicals, one was a historical center of evangelical strength (the United Kingdom, 11.6 million), but three had witnessed the growth of substantial evan-gelical populations mostly in the past century (India, 9.3 million; South Korea, 9.1 million; South Africa, 9.1 million). Of the remaining twenty-four countries where Barrett found at least one million evangelicals, only three were in Europe (Germany, Romania, Ukraine) and one in North America (Canada). Fully ten of these others were in Africa (An-gola, Congo-Zaire, Ethiopia, Ghana, Kenya, Mozambique, Rwanda, Tanzania, Uganda, Zambia), five were in Asia (China, Myanmar, In-donesia, Philippines, Australia), and five were in Latin America (Gua-temala, Haiti, Mexico, Argentina, Peru).

If Barrett's more diffuse categories of "Pentecostal," "charismatic," and "neo-charismatic" are employed, the world-wide distribution of evangelical-like Christian movements is underscored even more dra-matically.[18] In the enumeration of these categories, Brazil leads all the rest (79.9 million), followed then by the United States (75.2 million), China (54.3 million), India (33.5 million), South Africa (21.2 mil-lion), the Philippines (20.0 million), Congo-Zaire (17.7 million), Mexico (13.0 million) and then many other countries from Asia, Latin

---

[17]The encyclopedia defines "evangelicals" like this: "A subdivision mainly of Protestants con-sisting of all affiliated church members calling themselves Evangelicals, or all persons belong-ing to Evangelical congregations, churches or denominations; characterized by commitment to personal religion."

[18]There is some overlap in the encyclopedia's enumeration between these three categories and the "evangelical" category. The *Encyclopedia's* definitions are as follows: "Pentecostals" = Ad-herents of traditional Pentecostal denominations. "Charismatics" = "Baptized members af-filiated to nonpentecostal denominations who have entered into the experience of being filled with the Holy Spirit; the Second Wave of the Pentecostal/Charismatic/Neocharismatic Re-newal." "Neocharismatics/Independents" = Members of the Third Wave of the Pentecostal/Charismatic Renewal characterized by the adjectives Independent, Postdenominationist and Neo-Apostolic.

America and Africa, as well as Europe.

These tables, when combined with summary accounts of American missionary personnel, bring the key interpretive questions to the fore: Did the American missionary movement cause the expansion of Christianity outside the United States? More particularly, is the rise of nondenominational, evangelical and Pentecostal proportions within the American missionary force the best explanation for the very rapid rise of nondenominational, evangelical and Pentecostal believers elsewhere in the world?

Stating the questions so baldly almost instinctively rules out the answer that American Christians directly and comprehensively dictated the shape of the new world Christianity. Not only would such a picture have to ignore such obvious facts as the world's more than one billion Roman Catholics, whose outside influences are much more likely to come from the Vatican than from Chicago, Atlanta or Los Angeles. It would also have to play down the multiplied millions of local decisions made by indigenous believers over long periods of time in favor of the thousands of missionary actions taken by Americans (and a rapidly growing number of non-American missionaries) over much shorter periods.

If conclusions about American dominance of worldwide Christianity are preposterous, conclusions noting American influence are more plausible. If observers recognize that such influence has been exerted in greatly different measures in the world's rapidly multiplying Christian communities, it does make sense to talk of an American factor in world Christianity as it has come to exist.

In particular, it is important to stress that American missionary influence increasingly reflects forms of Christian faith that are conversionist, voluntarist, entrepreneurial and nondenominational. To the extent that these forms of Christianity possess an affinity with the rapidly changing economic, demographic, social and cultural character of the world itself, we have a partial explanation for how and why American missionary efforts have helped shape world Christianity.

But if this observation holds, it complicates the interpretation of American influence. The ability of Americans, especially evangelical

Americans, to exploit voluntary and entrepreneurial Christianity helps explain the weight of American influence in a world increasingly marked by voluntary and entrepreneurial culture. But voluntary and entrepreneurial Christianity is a much more fluid type of the faith than centralized, strongly denominational and carefully structured forms of Christianity. Thus, when Americans promote less traditional forms of Christianity, they encourage local Christianities less amenable to the usual lines of ecclesiastical, intellectual or institutional control from abroad. American missionaries, in other words, have increasingly come to promote a Christian faith that makes it more likely, rather than less likely, for the believers they influence elsewhere to chart their own ways forward.

* * *

When considering world missionary forces today, one more important matter must at least be mentioned. That matter is the growing reality of missionary service defined as Christian believers going from everywhere to everywhere.[19] No one would deny the large impact of Americans on world missionary activity. But by early in the twenty-first century, the rising reality on the missionary horizon was the presence of non-Western missionaries increasingly active in all regions of the world. In numbers we have quoted before, over twelve thousand missionaries from both Brazil and Korea are now active outside their own borders. Probably, a comparable number of missionaries from the northeast Indian states of Nagaland and Mizoram are doing missionary work in other regions of India to the west and south. In Philip Jenkins's helpful recent study of Christianity in contemporary Europe, he cites the presence of over fifteen hundred missionaries from over fifty countries in Britain. Missionary organizations like the El Shaddai movement from the Philippines (a lay charismatic organization), the Christian Church Outreach Mission from Ghana (founded by Abraham Bediako) and the Kimbanguist church from the Democratic Republic of Congo are among the larger groups that also sponsor mis-

---

[19]For an insightful exposition of this theme, see Michael Nazir-Ali, *From Everywhere to Everywhere: A World View of Christian Witness* (London: Collins/Flame, 1991).

sionaries in dozens of European and some American locations.[20]

It would be foolish to deny a large role both for the United States and for American believers in the recent world history of Christianity. Even more foolish would be to think of American missionaries as the sole, or even the most important, engines driving the churches around the world.

---

[20]Philip Jenkins, *God's Continent: Christianity, Islam, and Europe's Religious Crisis* (New York: Oxford University Press, 2007), 89-91.

Indictment and Response

WHEN CONSIDERING THE QUESTION OF AMERICAN CHRISTIANS in relation to the rest of the world, a primary issue is whether missionaries from the U.S. have been principal agents of change or have only filled lesser and supporting roles. This question takes up a subject that is as complex as it has been understudied. The images of missionaries presented in American popular media are almost completely useless for answering the question, since their stock in trade is the emotive stereotype—whether, from different ideological angles, of innocence among primal peoples, repressed sexuality among mission imperialists, gnostic purity among missionary altruists, or some other purely Western type.[1] A quick glance at the situation for Russia and a longer examination of

---

[1]The film *Black Robe* (1991) was a rare exception to the stereotyping of missionaries and their work, as witnessed, for example, with great variation in *The Mission* (1986), *At Play in the Fields of the Lord* (1991), and *The Mosquito Coast* (1986), or in novels like John Grisham, *The Testament* (New York: Doubleday, 1979), and Barbara Kingsolver, *The Poisonwood Bible* (New York: HarperFlamingo, 1998). For an assessment, see Jay Blossom, "Evangelists of Destruction: Missions to Native Americans in Recent Films," in *The Foreign Mission Enterprise at Home: Explorations in North American Cultural History*, ed. Daniel H. Bays and Grant Wacker (Tuscaloosa: University of Alabama, 2003).

missionary activity among indigenous peoples suggest the status of current discussions and also show the need for more careful assessment of research already undertaken. But even they touch only indirectly the question of how much world Christian history is now being driven by American forces. It is one thing to ask how American missionaries have aided U.S. economic and political interests; it is another to ask why forms of Christianity resembling American evangelicalism in at least some particulars now flourish in so many parts of the globe. More scholarship, unfortunately, has been attempted on the first question than the second. This chapter again features evangelical efforts, but since evangelicals have provided most of the personnel and most of the creative efforts of recent missionary history, this focus may actually sharpen consideration of American influence overseas.

RUSSIA

A growing literature now exists to document the irritation of Russians at the influx of aggressive evangelical missionaries after the collapse of state communism ca. 1990. In the former Soviet Union alone, the number of foreign missionaries went within a decade after 1987 from a bare handful to over 3,000 career missionaries and almost as many short-term visitors. With the exception of 557 South Korean missionaries who were active in Russia by 1997, most of the new missionaries were from the United States, and virtually all of them were evangelicals of the conversionist, voluntarist sort. The result was a series of wounded accusations from the Russian Orthodox Church—the new missionaries were forgetting Russia's ancient Christian heritage, they were treating Orthodoxy as a species of infidelity, they were destroying authentic Russian patriotism, they proclaimed an inferior message of original sin and conversion in place of the historic Orthodox doctrine of theosis (divinization), they were securing evangelical conversions through money and gifts, and so forth. But were these mostly American missionaries actually making a difference? According to the most reliable accounts, some Russian Protestants were being strengthened by their contacts with the foreign missionaries, some new cooperation between the Orthodox and Protestants emerged, and some promising evangelical institutions were founded. But considering the size of the former Soviet Union, the relatively small number of new missionaries relative to the extent of Orthodox institutions and personnel (even after the destructions of the Soviet era), and the general spiritual malaise portrayed in many recent accounts of Russian society, it is difficult to view the recent presence of American evangelical missionaries as overwhelmingly influential.[2]

INDIGENOUS PEOPLES: INDICTMENT

A more substantial literature has grown up around charges from anthropologists, journalists and political progressives about American missionaries supporting American economic or political imperialism among indigenous peoples of Southeast Asia, Africa, the Philippines and especially Latin America. The charges, which have been circulating at least since the early 1970s, reprise similar accusations that were once a stock in trade among critics of earlier British missionary activity.[3] The most serious of the current charges contend that missionary complicity in U.S. imperialism has resulted in ethnocide, or the deliberate destruction of indigenous peoples. Sometimes the accusations have been leveled against evangelical and fundamentalist missionaries in general, sometimes against particular mission organizations. Among the latter, special attention has been paid to two interdenominational organizations. The first is New Tribes Mission, which was founded in 1942 in order to bring Christian evangelism and Bible translations to previously isolated tribal groups. The second is the Wycliffe Bible Translators, an overtly evangelical agency seeking to create Christian churches among tribal peoples around the world. A particular point of contention for critics of

---

[2]See especially Mark Elliott and Anita Deyneka, "Protestant Missionaries in the Former Soviet Union," in *Proselytism and Orthodoxy in Russia: The New War for Souls*, ed. John Witte Jr. and Michael Bourdeaux (Maryknoll, N.Y.: Orbis, 1999), 197-223 (with numbers of missionaries specified, 199-200, 221-22). See also Mark Elliott, "East European Missions, *Perestroika*, and Orthodox-Evangelical Tensions," *Journal of Ecumenical Studies* 33 (Winter 1996): 9-20; Michael J. Christensen, "Evangelical-Orthodox Dialogue in Russia on the Eve of the Tenth Anniversary of Chernobyl," *Journal of Ecumenical Studies* 33 (Winter 1996): 79-86; and the continuing coverage in a newsletter edited by Mark Elliott, *East-West Church and Ministry Report*.

[3]For thorough discussion, see Brian Stanley, *The Bible and the Flag: Protestant Missions and British Imperialism in the Nineteenth and Twentieth Centuries* (Leicester, U.K.: Apollos, 1990).

Wycliffe is that its personnel also staff the Summer Institute of Linguistics, a self-described scientific organization that offers its services to governments around the world for the purpose of studying, recording and transcribing previously unwritten languages.

A lengthy parade of substantial writing has made the charges of imperialistic ethnocide against these and similar missionary organizations.[4] The impetus for much of this literature was provided by a 1971 meeting in Barbados sponsored by the Programme to Combat Racism and the Churches Commission on International Affairs of the World Council of Churches, along with the Ethnology Department of the University of Bern, Switzerland. This gathering issued a "Declaration of Barbados: For the Liberation of the Indians" that called on all interested parties to end the destructive "acts of aggression directed against the aboriginal groups and cultures." The Declaration accused several Latin American states of promoting such acts and also implicated the work of missionaries, which "reflects and complements the reigning colonial situation." In particular, "The missionary presence has always implied the imposition of criteria and patterns of thought and behaviour alien to the colonised Indian societies. A religious pretext has too often justified the economic and human exploitation of the aboriginal population. The inherent ethnocentric aspect of the evangelisation process is also a component of the colonialist ideology."[5]

In the wake of the Barbados Declaration a rush of writing expanded on the document's analysis and reinforced its charges against missionaries. In 1976, for example, Richard Arens edited a collection, *Genocide in Paraguay*, whose eight essays chronicled what the book's contributors called the intentional destruction of the Aché Indians. Critics of this book were, however, quick to point out that only two of its authors had ever visited the Aché themselves.[6]

---

[4]For orientation to this literature, I am indebted to my Wheaton College friends, Kathryn Long and Dean Arnold, and also to the splendid literature review provided by Jeffrey D. Webster and Thomas N. Headland, "Selected Annotated Bibliography: Conflicts Between Missionaries and Anthropologists and A Review of Missionaries' Reported Involvements in Human Rights," *Missiology* 24 (April 1996): 271-80.
[5]"The Declaration of Barbados," *Current Anthropology* 14 (June 1973): 268.
[6]Richard Arens, ed., *Genocide in Paraguay* (Philadelphia: Temple University Press, 1976). For criticism, Webster and Headland, "Selected Bibliography," 271-72.

More substantial was a colloquy from 1981, *Is God an American? An Anthropological Perspective on the Missionary Work of the Summer Institute of Linguistics*. This book included studies of Wycliffe/SIL work among Indian tribes in Bolivia, Brazil, Colombia, Ecuador and Peru, and more general essays with titles like "The Summer Institute of Linguistics: Ethnocide Disguised as a Blessing" and "God is an American." The book's argument took the following lines:

1. "The vast majority of the world's unwritten languages are spoken by ethnic groups without long histories of integration into state-level societies."

2. The mission of Wycliffe/SIL is to reduce as many of these languages as possible to writing, to translate the Bible into these languages, and then to establish evangelical Christian churches among these groups. Wycliffe's rapid post-war expansion has made it a particularly important force among tribal groups, especially in Latin America.

3. Wycliffe's workers see themselves as fighting Satan. "Considering the social background of SIL members, [the] identification of Satan with Communism seems logical. Similarly there is an equally natural tendency for God to be transformed into an American."

4. Whether inadvertently or deliberately, Wycliffe/SIL, thus, perpetuates "the various injustices suffered by the Indians at the hands of traders, cattle ranchers, professional hunters, rubber collectors, gold prospectors, oil companies, the army and other state institutions. The underlying force behind these diverse forms of encroachment is capitalism's attempt to resolve its internal contradictions by appropriating the Indians' labor-power, land, and resources. . . . The pressures brought to bear on Indian societies have made political and humanitarian assistance for the indigenous groups urgently necessary. This has been the opening of organizations like SIL. The missionaries have exploited the situation to advance their own goals rather than improve the position of the Indians. . . . In trying to solve 'the Indian problem' SIL has become 'the Indian problem.' By implanting into Indian society its individualism and materialism, SIL has deprived them of exactly those social resources and values which

could prevent their being totally 'integrated' and destroyed. SIL's program tends to produce tribeless Bibles rather than Bibletribes. . . . The campaign against SIL is not against an organization that innocently translates Bibles, provides education or distributes medicine, but against its holy alliance with American ideology, international capitalism, and national 'development plans.'"[7]

This particular indictment featured several of the classic themes making up the last century's anti-Americanism. Thus, American individualism undercuts the communal solidarity of traditional societies; American materialism ruins less acquisitive ways of life; American capitalism turns its victims into aggressive manipulators of land, labor and leisure. Even more recently, critics of economic globalism add a further indictment by criticizing the American role in international trade, monetary flow and the never-ending quest for the cheapest labor markets.

A more evenly balanced statement of these early indictments of American missionary work, and Wycliffe/SIL in particular, appeared two years after the publication of *Is God an American?* It came from David Stoll, who had also contributed an essay to that earlier volume. His book was titled *Fishers of Men or Founders of Empire?*[8] Stoll was a trifle less alarmed about SIL serving as a running dog lackey for American ideology and international capitalism. Instead, he was more concerned about what he described as the duplicity of the Bible translators in presenting Wycliffe to North American supporters as a ministry of evangelism and SIL to Third-World governments as a scientific institution. Stoll worried especially that the latter activity often resulted in Wycliffe/SIL doing the bidding of right-wing oppressive regimes in the various countries in which it operated.

Throughout the closing years of the twentieth century, other authors provided variations on these same themes—whether accusing New Tribes Mission and Wycliffe/SIL of slave trafficking in league with the

---

[7]Quotations from Søren Hvalkof and Peter Aaby, "Introducing God in the Devil's Paradise," and "No Tobacco, No Hallelujah," in *Is God an American?* ed. Søren Hvalkof and Peter Aaby (London: International Work Group for Indigenous Affairs and Survival International, 1981), 9, 11, 185.
[8]David Stoll, *Fishers of Men or Founders of Empire? The Wycliffe Bible Translators in Latin America* (Cambridge, Mass.: Cultural Survival, 1982).

CIA,[9] charging the New Tribes Mission of raiding, capturing and imprisoning Ayoreode Indians of Paraguay in labor camps,[10] ascribing to the SIL a plot to destroy the Culina Indians' identity through the weapons of Western capitalism,[11] or finding a sinister conspiracy at work in connections between Nelson Rockefeller's Big Oil and the widespread connections of the Wycliffe founder, Cameron Townsend.[12] An especially important contribution to this general indictment was provided by the second and third editions of a widely read book by anthropologist Napoleon Chagnon on the Yanomami of Brazil and Venezuela, in which he portrayed missionaries to this tribe as essentially blind to the Indians' best interests:

> In most cases reason and dialogue were not possible, for the missionaries were incapable of viewing the differences between "good" and "bad" in anything other than narrow biblical or theological terms, and could not appreciate the argument that the wanton destruction of a culture, if not its human bearers, was morally "bad" by some standards. Evangelism was by definition "good" in their terms if only a single soul was saved, and any price was worth paying to accomplish that end and any method legitimate.[13]

An expansion of this standard critique, along with a shift in focus of its application, then appeared in a full-scale indictment offered by a team of sociologists and religionists who described a new global Christian fundamentalism in league with an aggressive international capitalism and targeting, not this time isolated tribes, but the rapidly growing populations of the world's new great cities. With these modifications,

[9]Norman Lewis, *The Missionaries: God Against the Indians* (London: Secker & Warburg, 1988). For comment, see Webster and Headland, "Selected Bibliography," 275-76.

[10]Ticio Escobar, *Ethnocide: Mission Accomplished?* (Copenhagen: International Work Group for International Affairs, 1989). For comment, see Webster and Headland, "Selected Bibliography," 274.

[11]Donald K. Pollock, "Conversion and 'Community' in Amazonia," in *Conversion to Christianity: Historical and Anthropological Perspectives on a Great Transformation*, ed. Robert W. Hefner (Berkeley: University of California Press, 1993), 165-97. Webster and Headland, "Selected Bibliography," 276, point out that Pollock never visited the Culina.

[12]Gerald Colby and Charlotte Dennett, *Thy Will Be Done: The Conquest of the Amazon: Nelson Rockefeller and Evangelism in the Age of Oil* (New York: HarperCollins, 1995).

[13]Napoleon Chagnon, *Yanomamö: The Fierce People*, 3rd ed. (New York: Holt, Rinehart and Winston, 1983), 205.

the authors' bill of particulars was just about the same: "For Christian fundamentalism in particular, the universalizing of the faith is intertwined with the homogenizing influence of consumerism, mass communication, and production in ways that are compatible with the creation of an international market culture by global capitalist institutions."[14] The authors do recognize that some of the best-known promoters of this kind of religion include non-Americans like Reinhard Bonnke of Germany and Paul Yongi Cho of South Korea. But they still track most of the money, energy and motive force of "global fundamentalism" back to the United States.

More recently, themes from these earlier indictments reappeared in public statements from Hugo Chavez, president of Venezuela, that criticized the work of American missionaries in his country. To Chavez, who directed his criticism explicitly against the New Tribes Mission, the missionaries were "imperialists" trying to promote "colonialism." About the only item new in Chavez' critique was the charge that the American government was using these missionaries to prepare a coup against his regime.[15]

INDIGENOUS PEOPLES: RESPONSE

The lengthy roster of works critiquing evangelical missionaries for promoting American-led global capitalism has stimulated an equally formidable defense of missionary activity. That defense is important for understanding the character of American evangelical activity in the world—and, by extension, the United States more generally. But whether such defenses, or the indictments to which they respond, offer major assistance in understanding the general course of Christianity in the non-Western world is a question that must be addressed separately after sketching the response.

The defenders of American missionary practice make their case in weaker and stronger forms. Responsible apologists almost always grant

---

[14]Steve Brouwer, Paul Gifford and Susan D. Rose, *Exporting the American Gospel: Global Christian Fundamentalism* (New York: Routledge, 1996), 3.
[15]"Chavez Moves Against U.S. Preachers," *BBC News*, December 10, 2005, http://newsvote .bbc.co.uk/mpapps/pagetools/print/news.bbc.co.uk/2 (accessed Jan. 30, 2008).

that missionaries have in fact sometimes acted unwisely by sometimes linking the Christian gospel to the politics of American government, promoting capitalist exchange, or upsetting previously isolated tribal groups. But apologists have also made a number of effective responses.

In the first instance, critics of those who criticize the missionaries have found it fairly easy to expose the latter's ideological blinders. It was, for example, not an evangelical publication but a mainline Protestant periodical that attacked the notion of a Rockefeller-oil-Wycliffe conspiracy in these scathing terms: "To call this book's logic specious would be too complimentary. It is replete with factual errors, logical inconsistencies, inflated language and historically unrelated facts. Only ideology or money (probably the former) could have motivated its authors to do such a hatchet job."[16] In one of most ironic reversals in recent intellectual history, the anthropologist Napoleon Chagnon, who spoke so dismissively of missionary insensitivity to indigenous cultures, himself later became the target of charges that, as an anthropologist, he assisted in the physical and cultural destruction of his jungle subjects.[17] It has also been pointed out shrewdly that the demonization of "global fundamentalism" resembles nothing so much as fundamentalist eschatology stood on its head. As Joel Carpenter has written in response to one of the indictments: "The book's outline thus oddly resembles the millenarian writings of the fundamentalists themselves. Both expect to see the world's commercial and financial systems controlled by a central power whether it is called the 'investment classes' or the Antichrist."[18] Most importantly, careful investigation of supposed missionary malfeasance from anthropologists who are Christians themselves or sympathetic to Christianity have convinced many neutral observers that much of the missionary bashing results not from research, but simply from ideology.[19]

---

[16]Elizabeth A. Cobbs, review of *Thy Will Be Done*, by Gerald Colby and Charlotte Dennett, *Christian Century*, November 1, 1995, 1022.

[17]The charge is made most extensively in Patrick Tierney, *Darkness in El Dorado: How Scientists and Journalists Devastated the Amazon* (New York: Norton, 2000); for perspective, see Clifford Geertz, "Life Among the Anthros," *New York Review of Books*, February 8, 2001, 18-22.

[18]Joel A. Carpenter, review of *Exporting the American Gospel*, by Steve Brouwer, Paul Gifford and Susan D. Rose, *Church History* 66 (December 1997): 886.

[19]See especially two landmark essays, and the largely convinced responses of other anthropolo-

Even more forthright defenses of missionary practice come from those who seek to demonstrate that missionaries have helped rather than harmed the missionized. There are now many examples of such arguments. Non-Christian Chinese scholars have bestowed tempered words of praise on Protestant missionaries for the educational, medical and technical assistance they brought to their country.[20] Students of Central America have pointed out that some American missionaries were and are strong advocates of indigenous human rights.[21] Other students of Latin American Indian tribes now conclude that contact with missionaries has led to significantly better physical, intellectual and social health for indigenous peoples.[22]

But the most compelling apologists for the missionaries have been those who take a broad view of recent world history. They admit that missionaries have often played a key role in integrating indigenous people into wider social, economic and political life. Yet they insist that, since this kind of integration has become all but inevitable for virtually all tribal peoples, it has been far better for the indigenous people that missionaries instead of other possible agents were carrying out this integration. The most well-reasoned response to Stoll's *Fishers of Men or Founders of Empire?* for example, was provided by a Wycliffe worker who admitted that "for me, man's relationship to God is the first principle of life," but who also argued that the Wycliffe message of evangelical Christianity provided the "best way to bring those changes necessary to end oppression and human exploitation" that beset the Indians. Moreover, reducing indigenous languages to writing and teaching people to use

---

gists appended to the essays, Claude E. Stipe, "Anthropologists versus Missionaries: The Influence of Presuppositions," *Current Anthropology* 21 (April 1980): 165-79; and Robert J. Priest, "Missionary Positions: Christian, Modernist, Postmodernist," *Current Anthropology* 42 (February 2001): 29-68.

[20]Shen Dingping and Zhu Weifang, "Western Missionary Influence on the People's Republic of China: A Survey of Chinese Scholarly Opinion Between 1980 and 1990," *International Bulletin of Missionary Research* 22 (October 1998): 154-58.

[21]John Paul Lederach, "Missionaries Facing Conflict and Violence: Problems and Prospects," *Missiology* 20 (Jan. 1992): 11-19. For comment, see Webster and Headland, "Selected Bibliography," 275.

[22]Paul R. Turner, "Religious Conversion and Community Development," *Journal for the Scientific Study of Religion* 18 (1979): 252-60. For comment, see Webster and Headland, "Selected Bibliography," 279.

their own printed languages provided a means of protecting such people from the totalizing forces of modern civilization: "The group that is forced into isolation from the rest of society through illiteracy is defenseless before the crush of 'civilization'; it is destined for destruction."[23] The issue was put even more sharply by a veteran missionary in Irian Jaya (New Guinea): "Naive academics in ivy-covered towers may protest that the world's remaining primitive cultures should be left undisturbed, but farmers, lumbermen, land speculators, miners, hunters, military leaders, road builders, art collectors, tourists, and drug peddlers aren't listening. They are going in anyway. Often to destroy. Cheat. Exploit. Victimize. Corrupt. Taking, and giving little other than diseases for which primitives have no immunity or medicine. . . . We missionaries don't want the same fate to befall these magnificent tribes in Irian Jaya."[24]

Perhaps the most impressive statement of this argument was made in the late 1980s by an anthropologist who, in fact, criticized severely the work of New Tribes Mission with the Yuqui people of Bolivia. That criticism notwithstanding, Allyn Stearman's conclusion was a strong, albeit round-about, defense: "Had the Yuqui not been contacted by the New Tribes missionaries, the only people at the time willing to risk their lives in this process, it is certain that they would have been killed off or taken as [slaves]. . . . The fact of the matter is that very few people who do not have the driving zeal of the missionary are willing to put their lives on the line in a contact effort and to then devote the remainder of their existence to the difficult process of acculturation."[25] In a word, if the realm of the possible is limited to beneficent integration or destructive integration, missionary-led integration usually turns out to ·look beneficent.

---

[23]James Yost, "We Have a Mandate," *The Other Side* (February 1983): 25, 38. Yost was responding to David Stoll, "Wycliffe Bible Translators: Not Telling the Whole Story," ibid., 20-25.

[24]Don Richardson, "Do Missionaries Destroy Cultures?" in *Tribal Peoples and Development Issues: A Global Overview*, ed. John H. Bodley (Mountain View, Calif.: Mayfield, 1988), 117.

[25]Allyn MacLean Stearman, *Yuqui: Forest Nomads in a Changing World* (New York: Holt, Rinehart and Winston, 1989), 142, quoted in Webster and Headland, "Selected Bibliography," 277-78. For a superb account of how a nonbelieving anthropologist and the New Tribes Missionaries were later able to work together on behalf of the Yuqui, see Stearman, "Better Fed Than Dead: The Yuqui of Bolivia and the New Tribes Mission: A 30-Year Retrospective," *Missiology* 24 (April 1996): 213-26.

DISCUSSION

Convincing as apologies have been for missionary activity, however, they do not directly answer the question of how much American missionaries have affected the expansion of Christianity in the non-Western world. For that question, a still broader perspective is necessary. As a growing corps of solidly researched and carefully argued works is demonstrating, whether or not missionaries have acted wisely, the primary agency in recent movements of Christianization has not been the missionaries but the new converts themselves.

One of the strongest points made repeatedly in this literature is that it requires unusual hubris—among both supporters of American missionaries and their detractors—to presume that Westerners are primarily responsible for the recent mass expansion of non-Western Christianity. It is useful to add a few more examples to the roster already provided in chapter five. Thus, from the beginning of Western contact, when the Yoruba of Nigeria accepted Christianity, they did so in the context of Yoruba problems and for Yoruba solutions.[26] As the China Inland Mission made its way deep into China during the last third of the nineteenth century, Western publications highlighted the heroism of the CIM's missionaries, but on the ground the real advance took place when Chinese like Pastor Hsi Liao-chih effectively promoted the gospel.[27]

Among the vast, incredibly diverse panoply of African Independent Churches (AIC), it is probably possible to find a few that take their marching orders from outside sources. But as a burgeoning literature records, these AICs are much more often genuinely independent—in how they join Christianity to traditional African religion, in how they practice Christianity in the context of their own existing social conditions, and in how they apply Christianity to plan for the future.[28] More

---

[26]J. D. Y. Peel, *Religious Encounter and the Making of the Yoruba* (Bloomington: Indiana University Press, 2000).

[27]Alvyn Austin, *China's Millions: The China Inland Mission and Late Qing Society, 1832-1905* (Grand Rapids: Eerdmans, 2007).

[28]See, among many others, Allan Anderson, *Zion and Pentecost: The Spirituality and Experience of Pentecostal and Zionist/Apostolic Churches in South Africa* (Pretoria: University of South Africa Press, 2000); and Martinus L. Daneel, *African Earthkeepers: Wholistic Interfaith Mission* (Maryknoll, N.Y.: Orbis, 2001).

generally, as Philip Jenkins has recently asserted, "there must have been a great deal more to Southern Christianity than the European-driven mission movement," or that Christianity would have contracted when European colonization came to an end. "We can suggest all sorts of reasons why Africans and Asians adopted Christianity, whether political, social, or cultural; but one all-too-obvious explanation is that individuals came to believe the message offered, and found this the best means of explaining the world around them."[29]

To return to the emphasis placed by Lamin Sanneh on the effects of translation, it is his clearly phrased conclusion that Christianity's cross-cultural history always belongs in the forefront of attention. This cross-cultural dimension of Christianity, in fact, reveals something foundational about its character:

> The characteristic pattern of Christianity's engagement with the languages and cultures of the world had God at the center of the universe of cultures, implying equality among cultures and the necessarily relative status of cultures vis-à-vis the truth of God. No culture is so advanced and so superior that it can claim exclusive access or advantage to the truth of God, and none so marginal and remote that it can be excluded.[30]

Much good can come from analyzing carefully the actions of American missionaries overseas. What such analysis is less and less likely to discover is that American missionaries, whether for good or for ill, have been the controlling, hegemonic or sovereign agents of change in the recent world history of Christianity.

---

[29]Jenkins, *Next Christendom*, 42, 43-44.
[30]Lamin Sanneh, *Disciples of All Nations: Pillars of World Christianity* (New York: Oxford University Press, 2008), 25.

American Experience
as Template

THE BEST CONCLUSION TO BE REACHED AT THIS POINT in time about the relation of American Christianity to world Christianity is a modest one. In recent decades world Christian movements, especially Protestant and independent movements, have come increasingly to take on some of the characteristics of American Christianity. Yet the primary reason for that development is not the direct influence of American Christians themselves. It is rather that social circumstances in many places of the world are being transformed in patterns that resemble in crucial ways what North American believers had earlier experienced in the history of the United States (and to a slightly lesser extent in Canada). Without discounting the importance of direct American involvement around the world, the appearance of Christianities similar to forms of American Christianity highlights parallel development rather than direct influence.

To spell out that conclusion, this chapter draws on the work of two unusually perceptive scholars, the missiologist Andrew Walls and the social theorist David Martin. It then explores two ways of extending the insights of these scholars—first by noting how foreign observers have characterized the development of Christianity in the United States and then, through the work of an African historian, Ogbu Kalu, by examining the worldwide spread of Pentecostalism as connected to, but never dominated by, American developments.

THE MAIN POINT

The main point I am trying to make depends heavily on the insights of Andrew Walls, who has consistently produced the most insightful interpretations of the new shape of world Christianity. In several essays, Walls suggests that the nineteenth century witnessed two developments that were of extraordinary significance for later world history.[1] First was the successful adaptation of traditional European Christianity to the liberal social environment of the United States. Second was the emergence of the voluntary society as the key vehicle for Protestant missionary activity. As we have seen from the record of missionary endeavor by American Protestants, these developments were obviously linked. By the start of the twentieth century, American Protestants were well along the way to making voluntary missionary activity a great engine of evangelism and church organization that has now become standard in much of the rest of the world.

Yet something more needs to be said about both American history and the history of voluntary societies. The place to start is the late 1700s and an awareness of what happened in the United States during the century that followed.[2] During that period the United States experienced one of the most dramatic expansions of Christianity that to that

---

[1]See especially Andrew Walls, "The American Dimension of the Missionary Movement," and "Missionary Societies and the Fortunate Subversion of the Church," in *The Missionary Movement in Christian History: Studies in the Transmission of Faith* (Maryknoll, N.Y.: Orbis, 1996), 221-40, 241-54; and "The Missionary Movement: A Lay Fiefdom?" in *The Cross-Cultural Process in Christian History: Studies in the Transmission and Appropriation of Faith* (Maryknoll, N.Y.: Orbis, 2002), 215-35.

[2]For an expansion of this account, see Mark A. Noll, "'Christian America' and 'Christian Canada,'" in *The Cambridge History of Christianity*, vol. 8, *World Christianities, c. 1815-c.1914*, ed. Sheridan Gilley and Brian Stanley (Cambridge: Cambridge University Press, 2006), 359-80.

time had ever taken place in the long history of the church. From 1815 to 1914, the U.S. population grew very rapidly (from 8.4 million to 99.1 million). Yet over the same century Christian adherence grew even faster, from under one-fourth of the population to over two-fifths of the population, that is, from something around two million to something around forty million. Only the recent history of Christianity on the continent of Africa and in China reveals a more rapid increase of Christian adherents in a single geographical location.

As a comparative footnote, it is pertinent to observe that during the same nineteenth century, Canada, though with a smaller population, experienced proportionally an even greater Christian expansion than the U.S.—from maybe one-fifth church adherence in a population of 600,000 to one-half in a population of 8,000,000.

Yet striking as these nineteenth-century numerical increases were, something more important than mere numbers was at work. As Andrew Walls has drawn the picture, an immensely significant development was the American turn toward voluntary, self-directed organization as the dominant means for carrying on the work of the church.[3] For the most part, American believers practiced the faith by forming their own churches and religious agencies, generating their own financial support, and taking responsibility themselves for spreading and upholding the faith. For the most part, voluntarism became the pattern for all churches in America, whether the older state-churches of Europe (Catholics, Episcopalians, Presbyterians, Lutherans, English Puritans), Europe's Dissenting traditions (Baptists), or the newer Christian movements of the modern period (Methodists, Disciples, independents of many varieties). To be sure, the pattern of self-starting, self-financing and self-spreading Christianity had been anticipated by significant earlier movements—for example, some of the most independent-acting monks and friars of the Middle Ages, European pietists in the seventeenth and eighteenth centuries, and eighteenth-century British evangelicals who responded to the preaching of John

---

[3]A key book for the interpretation that follows and that complements Andrew Walls's work in many places is Nathan O. Hatch, *The Democratization of American Christianity* (New Haven: Yale University Press, 1989).

Wesley in England, Howell Harris in Wales and George Whitefield all over the Atlantic world. But this voluntary pattern came into its own during the nineteenth century as American believers used the powerful (if also sometimes fragmenting) resources of liberal democracy to establish and support their churches.

Historically, Eastern Orthodoxy, Catholicism and the major European Protestant denominations had differed substantially among themselves, but almost all assumed that Christianity required Christendom—which meant taking for granted formal cooperation between church and state as well as a prominent place for the churches in the formal legal life of a society. It also meant that great weight was given to historical precedents—how things should be done depended as much on previous patterns as upon assessments of current opportunities. In short, Christendom meant that society was intended to function as an organic whole, with comprehensive public acknowledgment of God and comprehensive religious support for the nation.

The new American pattern did not abandon the Christendom ideal entirely, but it nonetheless embodied a much more informal Christianity and pushed consistently for ever-more-flexible institutions and ever-newer innovations in responding to spiritual challenges. To be sure, a great deal of traditional European faith survived in America, especially among the Lutherans, Episcopalians, Roman Catholics, Eastern Orthodox and some of the Calvinistic denominations that continued to value their European roots. But even in these groups, the voluntary principle worked with unprecedented effects. In many Christian traditions it became completely dominant.

In North America, the addition of a voluntary mindset to what had been inherited from Europe was remarkably successful in evangelizing the people and then bringing a measure of Christian civilization to wide-open, frontier America. An elective affinity grew between the kind of Christianity that became so important in the American setting and the American social movements in which it flourished—between, that is, a conversionistic, voluntaristic form of Christian faith, and fluid, rapidly changing, commerce-driven, insecure and ethnically pluralistic social settings. Almost all American churches in the nineteenth century grew at a much faster rate than the American population as a whole. They did so by adapting what they had brought from Christian Europe to the much looser cultural conditions of the new world.

ALTERNATIVE EXPLANATIONS

A key interpretive question for recent world history asks why this type of Christianity has now become so widely spread and so dynamic around the globe. The first and (to some) most obvious explanation is that American traits have spread because American influence has spread. That influence can be traced, for example, in military and diplomatic history. The United States' defeat of Spain at Manila Bay in the Philippines (1898) won the world's attention for a nation that had once been regarded as only an isolated set of former British colonies. The boost given to the Allies by the United States' late entry into World War I (1917) further enhanced the United States' international standing. Then its leadership of the war effort against Germany and Japan (1941-1945), its key role in winning the global Cold War against Communism (1945-1989), and its recent invasions of Iraq (1991 and 2003) demonstrated the United States' place as (or ambition to be) the world's leading military power. Even more than military influence, the United States' cultural and economic clout has continued to expand and broaden, despite stiff new competition, into the twenty-first century. Although the rapidly expanding economies of China, India and other non-Western countries point to a different pecking order for the future, the global reach of the United States in the early years of the twenty-first century remains second to none.

For the development of world Christianity, missionary history offers a revealing parallel to military and economic history. As we saw in detail above, early in the twentieth century American missionaries made up only about a quarter of the world Protestant total. In 1972, it was almost two-thirds. Moreover, as the twentieth century progressed, the character of the American Protestant missionary force shifted dramatically away from the traditional denominations, which retained some of the older instincts of Christendom. In their stead arose the newer evangelical faith-mission organizations, among which Christendom instincts were all but extinguished.

Without placing too much weight on mere numbers, it is important to note in passing that one of the major differences between Catholicism and Protestantism concerns the origin of missionaries. Where the twentieth-century worldwide Protestant missionary force was dominated first by Britons, and then increasingly by Americans, the worldwide Catholic missionary force for the first two-thirds of the century was dominated by Europeans from countries like Ireland, Italy and Belgium. Then in the last third of the century it was increasingly staffed by missionaries from the Philippines, India and other non-Western locations.

Again, as a comparative note, it is striking that Canada, with its smaller population, contributed an even larger proportion of its population to missionary service than did the United States. So in terms of worldwide missionary activity, the changes at work in the nineteenth and twentieth centuries have been a North American phenomenon, rather than merely a product of United States initiatives, and they have been worked out differently for Catholics as compared to Protestants.

If the focus remains on just the United States, however, there seems to be a straightforward and obvious explanation for much of the recent world history of Christianity: American variants of the faith—especially Protestant forms—have become important around the world because both the United States and the American missionary force became so important around the world.

As self-evident as this conclusion might appear, it is almost certainly not the most important reason for explaining why American styles of voluntary and entrepreneurial religion have become so important worldwide. Rather, the better explanation for the rise of American-style variants of Christianity concerns not direct American influence but the shape of life throughout the non-Western world. Christianity in various forms is now advancing rapidly in parts of the world where the instincts of ancient Christendom are largely absent. In addition, more and more societies have begun to take on at least some characteristics similar to what emerged in nineteenth-century American society.

These characteristics are especially obvious in the burgeoning cities of the Global South and in the rural areas worldwide that are being reshaped by global economic forces. These newer societies tend to be competitive and not deferential, open to Christian witness but not officially Christian, allowing space for entrepreneurial activity while not restricting religious expression too drastically. To the extent that these conditions have developed, it is not surprising that styles of Christianity that flourished in North America's competitive, market-oriented, rapidly changing and initiative-rewarding environment would also flourish when other environments begin to look more like nineteenth-century America than fifteenth-century Europe.

One of the world's leading students of contemporary world Christianity, the British sociologist David Martin, has commented shrewdly on connections between the acceleration of globalization and the world expansion of Christianity. By globalization, Martin means the "increasing speed of movement, as peoples, ideas, images, and capital take advantage of modern means of communication," especially as this speed has featured "the ability of capital to create an international economy." (This account also fits what happened in the United States during the nineteenth century.) As Martin describes it, modern globalization has been characterized by a tremendous take-off of urban population (replacing the traditional village), a tremendous explosion of available information (replacing restricted sources of knowledge), and a heightened sense of the self as an individual actor (replacing the self as defined by clan or historical setting).[4] When Martin turns to look at recent history, he notes that the cutting edge of Christian expansion has been broadly Protestant—often specifically Pentecostal. Or if it has been Catholic, it is Catholicism touched by some form of "modern" Christianity, whether the Catholic Charismatic Movement in Latin America or the Spirit-guided churches of Africa. Martin has observed that Pentecostalism in its nearly infinite varieties has expanded most rapidly where local conditions manifest a liberating, but also perilous, social tumult.[5]

---

[4]David Martin, "Evangelical Expansion in Global Society," in *Christianity Reborn: The Global Expansion of Evangelicalism in the Twentieth Century*, ed. Donald M. Lewis (Grand Rapids: Eerdmans, 2004), 273-77 (quotation, p. 277).

[5]See David Martin, *Tongues of Fire: The Explosion of Pentecostalism in Latin America* (Oxford: Blackwell, 1990); and *Pentecostalism: The World Their Parish* (Oxford: Blackwell, 2001).

If that affinity speaks to more than just American history, it provides a clue about the American role in recent world Christianity. Yes, American voluntaristic, conversionistic religion has certainly exerted an influence elsewhere. The more important reality, however, is not that world Christianity is being driven by American activity. It is, rather, that forms of conversionistic and voluntaristic Christianity have flourished where something like nineteenth-century American social conditions have come to prevail—where, that is, social fluidity, personal choice, the need for innovation and a search for anchorage in the face of vanishing traditions have prevailed.

The burden of this book is to suggest that what Martin describes as modern Christianity adapting to a globalizing world is similar to the process that took place in the United States when the churches of European Christendom adapted to the competitive, entrepreneurial, free-market American environment. If this parallel really has occurred, it means that American Christian experience is most important for the world not so much as a direct influence but as a template for recent Christian history.

Once again, missionary statistics may help to clarify the general situation. As table 7.1 suggests, while American interdenominational mission agencies have grown rapidly in recent years, the number of non-Americans working with the American agencies has grown much more rapidly. American-based agencies like Campus Crusade, New Tribes Mission and YWAM—as well as agencies that have always linked Americans with Canadians and the British (like Wycliffe, OMF, SIM)—now employ many times more non-Americans as full-time missionaries than Americans. These agencies must still count on Americans, but they are increasingly international in outlook and multinational in staffing. Most of the other large evangelical agencies (both denominational and nondenominational) enlist substantial numbers from outside the U.S. as well.

To be sure, these tables could suggest that American leadership is now being exercised through proxies. Yet the better explanation is that increasing numbers of non-Americans are choosing to work with organizations from the Minority World (U.S. and Europe) because they find

Table 7.1

U.S. and Non-U.S. Personnel in Evangelical Missionary Agencies, 1999/2001

	1999 U.S. Personnel	*2001 Total Personnel*	*2001 From Countries*	*2001 to Countries*
Denominationally based				
Southern Baptists	4,562	5,034	6	97
Assemblies of God (1914)	1,543	3,546	58	153
Christian & Miss. Alliance (1887)	726	1,652	17	61
Baptist Mid Missions (1920)	612	1,065	2	44
Baptist Bible Fellowship (1950)	755	905	1	79
Ass. Bapts. for World Evang. (1927)	716	850	3	46
Mission to the World—PCA	579	630	2	40
CBInternational (1943)	550	630	1	46
Church of the Nazarene (1908)	487	562	7	69
Interdenominational				
Campus Crusade for Christ (1951)	973	15,218	118	135
YWAM (1961)	1,817	11,808	132	144
Wycliffe Bible Translators (1935)	2,930	7,031	35	78
New Tribes Mission (1942)	1,514	3,073	32	31
Operation Mobilization (1957)	171	2,977	79	61
SIM (1893)	569	1,692	26	54
OMF International (1865)	156	1,245	23	32
TEAM (1890)	638	862	23	40
Frontiers (1972)	311	692	33	63

Sources: *Mission Handbook 2001-2003*, 51; *Operation World*, 743-46.

such work satisfying for their own reasons and in their own places.

Another set of numbers points in the same direction. A recent systematic compilation for evangelical and evangelical-like missionary movements worldwide shows that the ratio of local congregations to the missionaries that they send and support is now lower among the evangelical churches of over thirty countries than it is for evangelical churches in the United States. Thus, it is taking more American churches to field one missionary than churches in other parts of the world. For example, whereas there is one crosscultural missionary supported by every 0.7 evangelical churches in Singapore, by 2.1 churches in Hong Kong, 2.4 in Albania, 2.5 in Sri Lanka, 2.6 in Mongolia, 4.2 in South Korea, 4.9 in Myanmar, and 5.3 in Senegal, in the United States the ratio is 7.6 churches to one missionary.[6]

The proper conclusion from this flurry of numbers would seem to be that, while the United States contains a whole lot of evangelical churches, those churches are not now as proportionately active in cross-cultural missionary activity as many churches in the non-Western world. Evangelical dynamism in these other churches has replaced, or is replacing, the evangelical dynamism of American churches as the leading edge of world Christian expansion. That expansion seems to be tracking the earlier pattern of American adjustments to Christianity-after-Christendom.

FOREIGN OBSERVERS

Observations by foreign visitors concerning religion in the United States help put the relationship of American Christianity to world Christianity into clearer perspective. Such visitors regularly stress the effect of American circumstances in shaping the American practice of religion. Along the way, such observations also raise important questions about the spiritual quality of the faith that Americans have practiced, a subject to which we return in the book's last chapter.

In 1998, for example, a German visitor, Manfred Siebald, who teaches American studies at the Johannes Gutenberg University in Mainz, explained to a larger group of touring Germans why there were so many different Christian denominations in the United States. To Siebald, six factors were most important in shaping the United States' denominational plurality: the separatistic impulse, the division of church and state, immigration, westward movement, slavery, and revival movements.[7] Conspicuous by their absence in Siebald's account

---

[6]Patrick Johnstone and Jason Mandryk, *Operation World: Twenty-First Century Edition* (Waynesboro, Ga.: Authentic Media, 2001), 748-52. This compilation also shows a lower ratio of evangelical churches to missionaries for fifteen European countries and Canada than for the United States.
[7]For an expansion of Siebald's insights, see Mark A. Noll, *The Old Religion in a New World: The History of North American Christianity* (Grand Rapids: Eerdmans, 2002), 275-76; and Manfred

were the long-standing pillars of European Christendom, including a sense of tradition, respect for hierarchy or inherited authority, and communal identity defined by religious-ethnic heritage.

Another recent observer, Klauspeter Blaser of France, has also highlighted the way in which American concepts of religion reflect more general conventions of American life. In his view, American Christianity has been marked specifically by what he calls "a combination of Puritanism and the Enlightenment," which conceives of truth in terms of actions and tangible results more than as metaphysics or spirituality. Thought is oriented toward actualizing the person of the future, and that person corresponds to the ideal American."[8]

The French sociologist Sébastien Fath, who is also an active Baptist layman, offers a picture of American social history that complements Blaser's account of American intellectual history. In Fath's view, "a particularly Protestant heritage has profoundly shaped contemporary American society and the way in which Americans practice their social relationships." But in turn, "the social impact of a culture defined by choice" has decisively shaped the character of American Protestantism.[9]

A recent essay by Hartmut Lehmann adds an insightful comparison with German religious life. In addressing the question of why over the last two centuries the United States seemed to Christianize at the same time that much of Europe has dechristianized, Lehmann stresses the American combination of structural religious freedom and entrepreneurial religious activity:

> In the complex processes described here as christianization and dechristianization, in the United States and Germany, differences in the legal framework were effectively reinforced by differences in the religious context. In the United States factors such as voluntarism, revivalism,

Siebald, "Why It Is Difficult for European Observers to Understand the Relationship Between American Politics and Religion in the Twenty-First Century," in *Religion and American Politics: From the Colonial Period to the Present*, ed. Mark A. Noll and Luke E. Harlow (New York: Oxford University Press, 2007), 386-92.

[8]Klauspeter Blaser, *Les théologies nord-américains* (Genève: Labor et Fides, 1995), 14.

[9]Sébastien Fath, "Protestantisme et lien social aux États-Unis," *Archives de Sciences Sociales des Religions* 108 (October-December 1999): 5-24 (quotation, 6). For Fath's views in English, see "American Civil Religion and George W. Bush," in *Religion and American Politics*, 393-400.

and pluralism created a cultural climate which favored the growth of
religion and in which religious activism could easily be related to matters of justice and social reform. In Germany, factors such as the close
cooperation between state and church, the suppression of nonconform-
ism, and the domestication of active Christian groups produced a cultural climate in which religion was tainted with conservatism and with
opposition to "progress."[10]

All such observations repeat, in modern terms, what Alexis de Tocqueville said in his famous report from the 1830s on democracy
in America:

> On my arrival in the United States it was the religious aspect of the
> country that first struck my eye. As I prolonged my stay, I perceived the
> great political consequences that flowed from these new facts. Among
> us, I had seen the spirit of religion and the spirit of freedom almost al-
> ways move in contrary directions. Here I found them united intimately
> with one another: they reigned together on the same soil.[11]

SUMMARY TO THIS POINT

The analysis of Walls, Martin and the foreign observers points to a series
of conclusions about how American circumstances have shaped the expression of Christianity in America. What the foreigners often see more
clearly than Americans themselves is that American Christianity is un-
mistakably American as well as Christian. More generally, expressions
of religion in America—Catholic as well as Protestant, for other faiths
as well as Christians—have moved in the direction of these preferences:

- individual self-fashioning over communal identification

- a language of choice and personal freedom alongside a language of
  given boundaries and personal responsibility

- comfortable employment of commerce as opposed to cautious skepticism about commerce

---

[10]Hartmut Lehmann, "The Christianization of America and the Dechristianization of Europe
in the 19th and 20th Centuries," *Kirchliche Zeitgeschichte* 11 (1998): 12.

[11]Alexis de Tocqueville, *Democracy in America*, ed. and trans. Harvey Claflin Mansfield and
Delba Winthrop (Chicago: University of Chicago Press, 2000), 282.

- a conception of religious organizations as voluntary bodies organized for action instead of inherited institutions organized for holding fast

- an optimistic hope expressed in the creation of new institutions instead of a pessimistic skepticism about innovation

- personal appropriation of sacred writings over inherited or hierarchical interpretation of those scriptures

- a plastic, utilitarian attitude toward geography as opposed to a settled, geographically-determined sense of identity

- a ready willingness to mingle different ethnic groups (in at least public settings and despite America's wretched black-white history) as opposed to strong convictions about ethnic purity

- the innovations of the bourgeois middle classes instead of deference to traditional elites

When these traits appear elsewhere in world Christianity, it may be because American believers have been there to inculcate American ways of doing religion. It is more likely that local believers exhibit these characteristics because they are the means through which in their circumstances they embrace the realities of Christian faith.

GLOBAL PENTECOSTALISM AS A CASE STUDY

The standard picture of the momentous rise and spread of Pentecostalism in the modern world has a distinctly American flavor.[12] In this picture, various strands of American Christian faith came together under the force of unusual circumstances in the early twentieth century to ignite the distinctive Pentecostal fire that has now spread around the world. Those strands included Holiness teaching about the infilling of the Holy Spirit, Keswick emphases that spoke of "full surrender" to the power of the Holy Spirit, African American and Hispanic practice of a profoundly emotive faith, and convictions about the possibility of di-

---

[12]This summary of American events depends on scholars who do not make extravagant claims about American influence overseas: Edith L. Blumhofer, *Restoring the Faith: The Assemblies of God, Pentecostalism, and American Culture* (Urbana: University of Illinois Press, 1993); and Grant Wacker, *Heaven Below: Early Pentecostals and American Culture* (Cambridge, Mass.: Harvard University Press, 2001).

vine healing that were spread widely among many Protestants during the last decades of the nineteenth century.[13] When these strands came together under the effective preaching of leaders like Charles Parham, a Holiness advocate of entire sanctification, and William Seymour, a mild-mannered African American who taught listeners to expect the baptism of the Holy Ghost, the result was spiritual experiences of escalating intensity. These experiences culminated in a great revival beginning in 1906 at the Apostolic Faith Gospel Mission on Azusa Street in Los Angeles. In this revival the Holy Spirit's unmediated power was manifest in divine healing, visions, words of prophecy, and especially the gift of tongues as evidence of the Spirit's indwelling presence.

Then, in the standard picture, the news of events at Azusa Street spread rapidly, drawing visitors from Chicago, New York and the upper South who returned to their homes with new Pentecostal experiences and the new Pentecostal teaching. Before long, visitors from overseas were making the same pilgrimage with the same results. From Azusa Street, thus, spread the Pentecostal distinctives to the whole world. Soon American Pentecostal missionaries were themselves going overseas with the same message, and the revival spread farther and faster.

Skipping several decades, a last note is often appended to this standard account. Neo-Pentecostal movements, which have proliferated in recent decades, often promote a view of human faith as the key to bringing on divine bounty. Several important American healer-evangelists made up the vanguard after World War II in promoting these views. Now as they spread rapidly in Central America, Brazil, Nigeria, other parts of Africa, some regions of China, and more, it is easy to see a repeat of the Azusa Street era when American influences spread out to engulf the world.

This standard picture is not wrong so much as it is incomplete. Azusa Street did exert an influence in the world; contemporary neo-Pentecostal teachings did receive a real boost from the activity of significant American preachers; American influence did play an important role in pro-

---

[13]For an outstanding account of this widespread phenomenon, see Heather D. Curtis, *Faith in the Great Physician: Suffering and Divine Healing in American Culture, 1860-1900* (Baltimore: Johns Hopkins University Press, 2007).

moting a form of Christianity now embraced, according to the count of David Barrett and colleagues, by over 600 million believers around the world.[14]

But this picture is not the whole story. A significant recent study by the Nigerian scholar Ogbu Kalu has appealed for a new perspective on the development of "global Pentecostalism" which, as he describes it, looks different from an "African perspective."[15] In what follows I am drawing on Kalu's fine study in order to underscore the main points of this book.

Kalu wants to revise accounts that treat "world-wide Pentecostal churches [as] American outposts" or that picture the Majority World as a "blank tablet" waiting for new programming from America. He views these goals as necessary for a proper understanding of Christian history, but also as a response to critics, like those described in chapter six, who see evangelical or Pentecostal expressions anywhere in the world as a direct product of American economic, military or cultural hegemony. The long and complex argument of Kalu's pathbreaking study cannot be summarized easily, but the following highlights include some of his most important assertions.

- Regardless of where the spark came from that ignited Pentecostal movements around the world, these movements have almost always defined themselves as inspired by the Bible, especially accounts in the book of Acts about the Holy Spirit's direct power in the early church.

- The world's incredibly diverse range of Pentecostal expressions have been fed by many earlier streams of Christian thought, biblical interpretation and practice; some of them did originate in America, but many did not.

---

[14]David B. Barrett, Todd M. Johnson and Peter F. Crossing, "Missiometrics 2008," *International Bulletin of Missionary Research* 32 (January 2008): 30.

[15]Ogbu Kalu, "Modeling the Genealogy and Character of Global Pentecostalism: An African Perspective," *Ned Geref Teologiese Tydskrif* 47 (September-December 2006): 506-33. Kalu has explored such issues more broadly in *African Christianity: An African Story* (Trenton, N.J.: African World Press, 2007); *African Pentecostalism: An Introduction* (New York: Oxford University Press, 2008); and many other books.

- Most significantly, in many regions during the years, or even decades, before Azusa Street, Pentecostal-type phenomena were proliferating rapidly. As scholars quoted by Kalu put it for Brazil, Chile and Central America, "outside missionaries helped to spark, not create, a Latin American institution." In addition, significant revivals that can be seen as Pentecostal or Pentecostal-like movements took place in 1903 and 1906 (Korea), 1904 (Wales) and 1905-1906 (Mukti, India). These revivals received a boost, and may have been redirected in belief and practice once news of Azusa Street arrived, but they were well underway before that awakening in America took place.

- Moreover, the Pentecostal-type movements not connected in their early stages with Azusa Street exhibited certain emphases, especially the public confession of sin, that were never a prime feature of American Pentecostalism.

- In Africa, a whole series of churches, revivals and movements that now are rightly viewed as Pentecostal were up and running before Azusa Street, or, if they developed later, did so with a clearly African character. They were sparked by priestly figures like Nxele and Ntsikana among the Xhosa of South Africa; others arose in response to the prophetic ministries in West Africa of William Wadé Harris (1910-1914) and Garrick Braide (1914-1918); some came to life between the two world wars in reaction to European colonial rule; and still others arose later as spiritual responses to distinctly local conditions.

- In the 1960s, charismatic gifts began to appear among some Nigerian Roman Catholics, but without guidance from Catholic charismatics in the U.S. or Britain. They were directed rather toward countering the charismatic influence of African Independent Churches.

- In Africa, further, Pentecostals usually practice a Christian faith that responds directly to issues like "witchcraft, deliverance, healing, and prosperity (money and children) [that] emanate from the world-views and goals of indigenous religions."

- Crucial for the argument of this book, Kalu stresses that in recent decades the forces of economic globalization have created circumstances marked by "oases of wealth in the desert of scorching poverty, class conflicts, legitimacy crises, and . . . stunted populations." Against these conditions, the Pentecostal stress on the immediate presence of a loving God and the immediate work of an all-powerful Holy Spirit make for a Christianity with dramatic appeal.

In sum, Kalu insists on an account of global Pentecostalism that takes the global diversity of Pentecostal movements with utter seriousness. For his particular context, he stresses that African Pentecostalism must be viewed first in terms of African history before it is connected to American history. His word for historians is that "Pentecostal historiography must abandon the search for founding missionaries in nonwestern contexts." His word that is most relevant for this book is just as direct: "the American connection is more important in studying the character of the movement . . . than in tracing its genealogy." This fresh account of global Pentecostalism supports a general picture of Christianity as a world religion, with many connections between nations, but with no one nation as the controlling force.

*   *   *

As a believer, I ascribe both the spread and vitality of Christianity around the world to forces intrinsic to the faith itself. Christianity attracts adherents because Christianity is true. In historical perspective, however, it is also not difficult to see that the inner force of this religion—in Christian terms, the work of the Holy Spirit—has assumed many different forms in many different cultures, of which the voluntaristic conversions of American evangelicalism is only one. Yet in the modern world, where so many regions have come to experience social circumstances resembling, at least in some measure, the social experiences of American history, it is not so much American Christianity, but rather forms of Christianity analogous to what Christianity has become in the United States, that are rising in the world.

8

American Evangelicals
View the World, 1900-2000

WITH THIS CHAPTER WE BEGIN A SERIES OF THREE CASE
studies that expand upon the perspectives of the book. This one looks at
developments within the United States, the next examines Korean Christianity in relation to American Christianity, and the third probes the
extent of Western influence in the East African Revival. Together, they
broaden the consideration of Christianity in the United States in relationship to Christianity in the rest of the world, and in so doing prepare
the way for the concluding reflections of the book's last chapter.

The question of U.S. influence in the world also involves a question
about how Americans perceive the world.[1] This chapter, again focusing
on evangelicals, takes up that second question. It shows that when
American evangelicals have looked at the world, they have done so with
a mix of realism and romanticism; they have mingled careful attention
to what is out there with simple projections of what is happening here.

---

[1]For the preparation of this chapter, the extensive assistance of Jeffrey Gustafson, who patiently
scoured the periodicals and intelligently organized what he found, was indispensable.

A survey of how American evangelicals in the twentieth century saw the world reveals only a little self-conscious reflection on the great transformation in global Christianity that has taken place in the recent past. It does, however, testify to the ongoing engagement of American Christians with the world.

Even more, it documents what can only be called a loose relationship between what American evangelicals considered most important in the world and what was actually going on. This case study is not intended to stress the irony in American perceptions of the world or to charge evangelicals with myopic shortsightedness. It is intended, rather, to show that the story of evangelical attention to the lands beyond American borders makes up only a part, and sometimes only a small part, of the world's emerging Christian realities.

Stereotypes abound concerning the attitudes of United States citizens toward people and events in other parts of the globe. Thus, for example, Americans are blissfully ignorant of life beyond their own shores; Americans are interested only in the part of the world from which they or their ancestors came; Americans will go anywhere and do anything to defend human freedom; Americans are ugly bullies whose lust for profit abroad regularly undermines the integrity of local cultures; and so on.

A similar group of stereotypes is easily gathered with respect to the attitudes of Christian believers in the United States toward the fate of their religion in the rest of the world. These stereotypes include claims like the following: No national religious community gives so much money so freely as American believers to spread the gospel or to aid victims of natural disasters; no national religious community is so self-centered and self-contained as American Christians; American believers naturally assume that normative Christian practice in other parts of the world must look like normative Christian practice "at home"; because the United States has absorbed so many different strands of Christian tradition, its churches instinctively promote healthy forms of Christian internationalism; American Christians are blissfully ignorant about Christian life beyond their own shores; and so on. Stereotypes are repeated in part because they approximate some aspects of the truth. But to move beyond the blithe certainties of stereotyping, research will always be necessary. This chapter brings a modest, but specific, quantity of research to bear on the question of how, over the course of the twentieth century, American evangelicals perceived the broader picture of Christianity throughout the world.[2]

This chapter outlines a history of American evangelical attitudes toward worldwide Christianity by examining the editorial material found in three different publishing streams for each of five different years: 1900, 1925, 1950, 1975 and 2000. The streams are, first, magazines published by Moody Bible Institute (for all five years); second, centrist nondenominational magazines aimed at broad evangelical audiences (*Sunday School Times* for 1925 and 1950; *Christianity Today* for 1975 and 2000); and, third, magazines with Holiness and Pentecostal constituencies (*Free Methodist* for 1900, the *Pentecostal Evangel* for 1925, 1950 and 1975, and *Charisma and Christian Life* for 2000). Sampling only fourteen annual cycles of articles, reports, letters and editorial commentary spread over a whole century (the *Sunday School Times* for 1900 was not available) provides an admittedly incomplete picture. But even an incomplete picture grounded in research offers a better guide than mere stereotyping. After describing in some detail the magazines and what they reported about world Christianity in their various annual runs, the chapter summarizes the geographical focal points of American evangelical interest, describes the presence of national voices, assesses the prevailing framework for viewing the rest of the world, and closes with comments on the major changes noted over the course of the century. The net result suggests that there is some truth in nearly all stereotypes about American evangelical attitudes toward the world, but also that a closer look at these periodicals reveals much more than merely the stereotypes.

---

[2]For an earlier study that covers a little bit of the same ground, see Ortha May Lane, *Missions in Magazines: An Analysis of the Treatment of Protestant Foreign Missions in American Magazines Since 1810* (Tientsin, China: Tientisn Press, 1935)—my thanks to Elesha Coffman for this reference. A broad overview of how missionary service has reflected back on North American perceptions of the world is provided by Daniel H. Bays and Grant Wacker, eds., *The Foreign Missionary Enterprise at Home: Explorations in North American Cultural History* (Tuscaloosa: University of Alabama Press, 2003).

THE MAGAZINES AND THEIR COVERAGE

In 1900 the school now known as the Moody Bible Institute had just taken that name (changed after the death in 1899 of its founder, D. L. Moody, from the Bible Institute for Home and Foreign Missions of the Chicago Evangelization Society). Also in 1900 it issued the first numbers of its own magazine, *The Institute Tie*, which would later become the widely circulated *Moody Monthly* (which ceased publication only in 2003). In the first year, the *Institute Tie* ran only three features on international subjects, but former students reporting back on their places of service also passed on a great deal of information about other parts of the world. Missionary reports predominated, but hints about indigenous aspects of worldwide Christianity also came from the Institute's international alumni who also contributed, including two from Japan and one from Norway. Reports in 1900 mentioned persecution in Chile and India, but not in China where the Boxer Rebellion was exacting a terrific toll of bloodshed among both Protestants and Catholics, nationals and missionaries.

In the weekly *Free Methodist* during 1900, regular reports mirrored stories found in the major newspapers of the day, and there were occasional editorials with an international focus, as on the Boer War in South Africa and the Boxer Rebellion in China. Most of the foreign coverage was not original, but missionaries from about a half-dozen stations around the world supplied regular reports that connected readers with far-distant localities. Much of the reporting was from India where famine stalked millions, including orphans and others cared for by Methodist missionaries. One missionary in South Africa also provided regular character sketches of the national Christians with whom he worked.

In 1925 *Moody Monthly* published six major articles on missions, three of which defended the cause of foreign Christian service against attacks on missionary endeavor, two warned about modernism corrupting missionary motivation, and one was a missionary report from Belgium. In the magazine's departments and correspondence, reports appeared on the activity of churches in Poland, Russia, China and East Africa, and there was a great deal of information from missionaries about their service abroad. The weekly *Sunday School Times* also contained a full roster of international articles and reports, but with attention to national Christians predominating over missionary reports. This publication profiled a few indigenous Christian leaders in China and Africa, including several reports on the Chinese General Feng and his Christian army who were becoming international Christian celebrities. Ernest Gordon's monthly survey of religious life and thought frequently mentioned suffering Christians around the world; his regular references to national Christian activities reflected a general pattern in the magazine. In the weekly *Pentecostal Evangel* (circulation over 21,000) the focus was more thoroughly on missionary activity, most often through letters from the field. Occasionally, stories about local converts were featured in these letters, including accounts of healings or baptism in the Spirit, but their standard fare concerned the missionaries' battles for converts, the bearing of international crises on missionary activity and the need for funds.

In 1950, and in the wake of the Second World War, all three magazines focused more attention on international matters than had been the case earlier. *Moody Monthly* featured many articles on Christians and churches outside the United States, including long stories on the growth of Protestantism in Latin America and the activity of Christians in Korea. It also devoted complete articles to the persecution of believers in Mexico and China. In news and correspondence sections of the magazine, missionary voices were more prominent, but even here considerable information was provided on local situations, including one report of a Chinese evangelist in Indonesia who had recently opened four new churches.[3] There were also several stories on the status of the churches in the two Germanies. Several reports and articles considered the new state of Israel, usually (but not exclusively) in connection with biblical prophecy.

Attention to the world throughout 1950 in the *Sunday School Times* and the *Pentecostal Evangel* was more heavily oriented to missionary reports, but these periodicals also contained a great deal of information

---

[3]This story was unusual in identifying the Chinese evangelist by name, Leland Wong, instead of a Western missionary as the key agent; *Moody Monthly*, September 1950, 28.

on many foreign parts of the world. In the *Sunday School Times*, stories offered a grab bag, ranging from how to teach children about missions to stories about famous missionaries, but also with news on growing churches in Portugal, Guatemala, China and Mexico. Ernest Gordon continued to employ clippings from around the world for his monthly column. In the *Pentecostal Evangel,* reports from missionaries, usually associated with the Assemblies of God, predominated, and there were many references to the new state of Israel, again usually with a prophetic interest.

In general for 1950, as reflected in these magazines, American evangelicals were increasingly aware of the globalization of Christianity, and they were beginning to pay attention to the persecution of believers in other parts of the world. Articles about Israel, Palestine and the fulfillment of prophecy in the Middle East made up a prominent part of the coverage.

By 1975 the international perspective was more than ever central to editorial treatment. *Moody Monthly* (near the peak of its circulation at 260,000) directed much attention to churches outside the United States, but its coverage involved less paragraph inches and less thorough reporting than in 1950. News reports often treated national concerns, alongside accounts of missionary activity, and they regularly offered stories of persecution in the Soviet Union, other parts of Communist Europe, Vietnam and Africa. The *Pentecostal Evangel,* which in 1975 was functioning more as a house organ for the Assemblies of God than earlier in its history, offered a regular monthly feature on a particular foreign country made up of reports from missionaries serving in that place. The magazine's news section covered stories of denominational interest alongside stories about national Christians and about general international events.

Christianity Today, which had come into existence in 1956 as a biweekly, ran five substantial articles in 1975 on the Christian situation outside the United States. Two articles treated theological movements—in India and in Latin America (liberation theology); two others featured African leaders describing the situation for churches in their continent; and one more detailed what could be known about the church in China during Mao's Great Proletarian Cultural Revolution. Two more articles dealt with missions, one examining the rapid expansion of short-term and non-professional missionaries and the other challenging Americans to consider the perils of cultural imperialism. *Christianity Today*'s "World-Wide News" section covered a great number of stories, including regular reports on persecution in Communist lands, but it also treated restrictions on religious liberty in anti-Communist South Korea.

By comparison with 1900, 1925 and 1950, the magazines in 1975 were printing fewer straight reports from missionaries, they were gathering their articles and reports from a wider range of international sources, they devoted more space to describing national Christian leaders, and they concentrated more consistently on the persecution of national believers.

In 2000 the emphases visible in 1975 were intensified. *Moody* (now a bimonthly with the name changed in 1990) ran two issues with an international focus, one on short-term missions and the other on persecution of Christians around the world; in another issue it provided a major article on the church in Russia. The monthly *Charisma* regularly featured reports on the work of the Holy Spirit in far-flung regions of the globe, with a concentration on miracles and evangelism. What missionaries were doing was prominent throughout these reports, but even more prominent were reports on the activities of national believers. The kind of story that in former years would have provided information about missionaries holding evangelistic meetings, hosting local conferences or coordinating relief efforts now more often featured national Christians carrying out these same activities.

During the same year *Christianity Today* (circulation over 160,000) printed long articles on the church in Brazil, Tibet and Palestine; it offered two general stories on Christian peacemaking around the world; and it featured a historical piece on black liberation movements in Africa. Stories about missions and missionaries included one on the role of women, another on short-term missionaries, a third challenging the credibility of missionary statistics and a fourth (the most traditional) on evangelism in Amsterdam. International news offered extensive coverage of Christian activities throughout the world, including many stories of persecution. Coverage was also extended to considering religious implications of upheaval in the former Yugoslavia and the expansion of China's economic contacts with the rest of the world.

Each of the magazines preserved its own ethos, each spoke to a different segment of the evangelical mosaic, and each offered its own level of coverage with its own set of particular concerns. Yet all of the magazines showed a clear movement away from missionary reports to material coming from national Christians. All also featured the persecution of local Christians much more than their counterparts had done earlier in the century. All also seemed more aware of cooperation between American churches and churches in other parts of the world. By the year 2000 there were even a few stories on international Christian connections that did not involve the United States, as, for example, accounts of Chinese Christians in Cuba and Japanese believers in Brazil. In addition, reporting on international Christian organizations, like the World Council of Churches and its predecessor agencies, as well as on more strictly evangelical organizations like the Lausanne Conference on World Evangelization (1974), testified to growing awareness of the wider world. In these trends it is clear that American evangelicals were, through different means and with different emphases, becoming more aware of realities in the international Christian community, but usually still with the United States as the presumptive hub of worldwide activity.

GEOGRAPHICAL FOCAL POINTS

In geographical terms, the wider Christian world for American evangelicals changed considerably throughout the course of the twentieth century. For the first fifty years, China and India were the countries that mattered most, although if the continent of Africa were considered as a whole, coverage for all African regions and countries probably equaled coverage for China and India. Over the second fifty years, while treatment of China continued to be strong, India began to fade from American evangelical consciousness. This shift in focuses reveals an important shift in emphasis. In the beginning of the century, missionary reports provided much of the magazines' editorial content. Since China and India were the sites to which most Protestant missionaries went, they received the most coverage, and often with parallel accounts of unreached peoples, exotic local customs and hardship created by warfare and famine. By 1950 coverage began to reflect more directly the situation of worldwide politics rather than just missionary activity. American Christian writers devoted great attention to the fate of the Chinese national church under a communist government. When the Cold War became a major fixation in the magazines, treatment of the persecuted church in China was a natural subject. India, of course, had also undergone a political change of first magnitude with the end of British colonial rule in 1947. Yet because the threat of governmental persecution in India was less pressing, and because India played an auxiliary rather than a prime role in the Cold War, it received far less press attention than China, where the government expelled missionaries and where underground churches offered scenes of high drama. In general, as the source of magazine coverage shifted from missionary reports to general news reports, China loomed larger while India began to fade.

Attention to Japan paralleled the situation for India. Although the Christian churches grew more rapidly in Japan after World War II than before the War, American press coverage was stronger in the years before 1940. (The exception was considerable press devoted to the effort of the Pocket Testament League to supply the Japanese with Bibles when requested to do so by the military governor of post-war Japan, General Douglas MacArthur.) By contrast, there was much more press coverage of the churches in Korea after 1950 than before, although attention to Korea seemed to be receding slightly by the year 2000.

Israel and the Middle East also became a focal point of much more evangelical interest from 1950 onwards. Mass migration of Jews during the 1920s had received earlier attention, but nothing on the scale of what occurred after the formation of the state of Israel in 1948. At the forefront of the surge of stories on the Middle East in 1950 was consideration of biblical prophecy, especially debates as to which elements of contemporary history were fulfilling which predictions. In 1975 and 2000, the broader Palestinian-Israeli conflict competed for attention with the fate of Israel considered by itself.

Awareness of Latin America, Africa and Europe remained fairly constant throughout the century. The amount of coverage in the magazines did not change greatly even when the source of stories shifted from missionary reports to more general news. Central Asia and the Pacific were the regions of the world receiving the least attention from 1900 straight through to 2000.

NATIONAL VOICES

Throughout the century, the voices of national Christians were most often heard as testimonies to the power of the gospel or to the labor of dedicated missionaries. By contrast, accounts of ordinary believers living in ordinary circumstances were quite rare. The steady diet of missionary reports featured stories of conversions and the effect of these conversions on the lives of new believers. Such stories both demonstrated God's power at work and provided prima facie justification for missionary enterprise. A typical account in 1925, from a missionary report in the *Pentecostal Evangel*, told how a Chinese girl became convicted of sin during a meeting, was struck down to the floor, began confessing her sin, was ministered to by others in attendance with Scripture, and finally rose to sing praise to God.[4] Seventy-five years later, *Christianity Today* repeated a similar story of an Ecuadorian man who, after falling on a cactus when he was inebriated, stopped drinking and then followed his wife in converting to Christ when he saw the change in her behavior.[5] Especially earlier in the century there were reports of new converts who traveled to the United States in order to testify here to the power of the gospel. In 1900 the *Free Methodist* told of one such occasion:

> Miss Lillvati Singh, A. B. of Lucknow India, was a striking figure at the conference. Dressed simply in a native costume she was easily distinguished from all others on the platform. Her address was delivered in faultless English and in a tone distinctly heard in all parts of the im-

---

[4]"Our Missions and Missionaries," *Pentecostal Evangel*, April 4, 1925, 10-11.
[5]John W. Kennedy, "Out of the Ashes: Dispatch Ecuador," *Christianity Today*, January 10, 2000, 67.

mense auditorium. A graduate of Miss Thoburn's school for women in Calcutta, she is a living example of what the gospel can do for the women of India. A few years ago a "weak thing," as their language characterizes women, without hope for this world or the next, now a queenly, refined, educated Christian woman, the equal in every respect of any of her more favored sisters of the west.[6]

Photographs with captions like "The Fruit of the Harvest" regularly appeared with such stories of missionary converts.

Testimonies from believers overseas were also often published as a way to strengthen the faith of American readers. In the parts of their magazines devoted to children, the *Sunday School Times* and the *Pentecostal Evangel* regularly printed stories that told of the exemplary faith of young people in new churches overseas. The same exemplary purpose was sometimes pursued with adults, as when *Moody Monthly* in 1975 printed the life story of a Palestinian Christian turned evangelist.[7]

By contrast to testimonies of conversion and of exemplary Christian behavior under unusual circumstances, information about the daily life of regular Christian believers was almost nonexistent. In one of the few exceptions, *Christianity Today* once offered a glimpse into the lives of Filipino women who had taken employment as domestic servants in Hong Kong in order to support their families in the Philippines. The article told of the strong faith shared by many of these women, how they worshiped together weekly, and how they tried to share their faith with their employers.[8]

The missionary reports that predominated in the earlier part of the century regularly stressed the recruitment of native workers and often paused to praise the effectiveness of such workers. Names and details were often sketchy, but missionaries repeatedly focused on their national colleagues, both to illustrate the spread of the gospel and to solicit funds for supporting the work of these nationals.

Stories focusing on the work of local pastors increased over the course

---

[6] *Free Methodist*, June 19, 1900, 4.
[7] James and Marti Hefley, "Anis Shorrosh: The Liberated Palestinian," *Moody Monthly*, December 1975, 25-28.
[8] "World Report," *Christianity Today*, October 3, 2000, 26-29.

of the century. The pastors about whom these stories were written usually had experienced unusual success in evangelism or in leading revivals. Sometimes they displayed great courage or exemplary Christian
character. Such was the case of the Hungarian minister who was fired
for uncovering a bribery scandal in the Free Church of Hungary.[9] Early
in the century nearly equal prominence was accorded the work of "Bible
Women," particularly in China. These Bible Women were described as
mature in the faith, though some could be quite young; they were often
trained at Bible institutes alongside male colleagues who became evangelists or pastors.

Over the course of the century, several national believers received
unusual attention in the American press as examples of noteworthy
Christian service. Although treatment never reached the celebrity attention accorded to a few Americans like Billy Graham, repeated stories on single individuals shone the limelight far beyond American borders. So it was that early in the century several articles defended the
Chinese war hero Marshall Feng after Feng resigned his position in a
political move, as a person of dedicated Christian commitment. These
articles also stressed the growing numbers in his army who were loyal
to both their Christian commitment and to their general. Likewise
early in the century, several stories highlighted the work of William
Wadé Harris, along with his fellow African, Apollo, for their work in
planting churches in the Ivory Coast. In India, Christian Sadhu Sun-
dar Singh was likened to St. Francis; of Singh it was reported that his
life manifested such holiness that it caused Roman Catholics to question whether there might be salvation outside their church after all.[10]

The national churches that stood out as most important in American reports were, unsurprisingly, churches in action. Good stories came
from hard-working ministries. Thus, after the Second World War, the
Sunday School Times told of a German deaconess who combined skills
in outreach and nurture as she cared for orphans in a French village,
enlisted older believers to help with their care, and mobilized the whole

---

[9]"News," *Christianity Today*, August 29, 1975, 44.
[10]Ernest Gordon, "Survey of Religious Life and Thought," *Sunday School Times*, July 4, 1925,
    430-31.

community for the works of reconstruction.[11] Not surprisingly, how-ever, evangelism was the ministry most frequently highlighted. The Moody periodicals, for example, featured stories about churches in Mexico and Cuba that were effective in children's evangelism in, re-spectively, 1975 and 2000.[12] Earlier the *Sunday School Times* had noted the extraordinary hospitality of local believers in preparing for a con-ference for five thousand Africans and thirty-six missionaries in the eastern Congo:

> Christians at Tundra had made ready for them, row upon row of native huts for their accommodation, gardens cropped and storehouses full. Dried elephant meat hung about the station. The grandest sight was the open-air church arranged with much effort under large mango trees, a cool place in hot weather. Seats were logs and there was a large platform with two organs, microphones and loud speakers making hearing pos-sible to the farthest corners of this magnificent church.[13]

Less common was the kind of report that appeared in *Christianity Today* in 2000 about pastor Uriel Tercero and his congregation in Nica-ragua who, along with the gospel, were also teaching organic and envi-ronmentally sound methods of farming.[14]

Throughout the century the American magazines took special care to note when national churches raised money for local ministries and for missionary events around the world. In 1975 *Christianity Today* reported that seven hundred Liberian Christians had pledged $8,721.51 for mis-sions at a time when the average yearly income in Liberia was only $125.00.[15] The goal of self-supporting churches remained paramount, and missionaries consistently reported on progress to that goal. The generosity of Christians in other parts of the world also served as a way of challenging American Christians to give more generously. To pro-

---

[11]Ernest Gordon, "A Survey of Religious Life and Thought," *Sunday School Times*, May 13, 1950, 408-9.

[12]"WorldWide News Report," *Moody Monthly*, May 1975, 8; "News: International," *Moody Magazine*, September/October 2000, 46-47.

[13]Ernest Gordon, "A Survey of Religious Life and Thought," *The Sunday School Times*, August 12, 1950, 682-83.

[14]"World Report," *Christianity Today*, August 7, 2000, 32.

[15]"News," *Christianity Today*, February 28, 1975, 42.

mote such efforts, the magazines sometimes ran stories about gifts collected in the churches of one country that were sent for relief in others.

Reports of healings and miracles were never unusually prominent, though they did appear occasionally in missionary reports and more frequently in Pentecostal periodicals. For example, in 2000 *Charisma* ran a regular stream of miracle stories from abroad; they included reports contained in longer articles from missionaries in Mozambique and Uganda about people being raised from the dead.[16] The Moody periodicals almost never published such reports. They and the *Sunday School Times* did, however, often relay accounts of providential assistance, as in the 1925 story from the *Times* of a Chinese matron at a faith missions home who was known as a woman of prayer and who on at least two occasions received desperately needed provisions at just the last moment.[17] In 2000, *Christianity Today* told its readers that in the rapidly growing church in Nepal, 40-60 percent of Nepalese Christians had become believers as a result of a miracle.[18] Similarly, *Charisma* reported that miracles were common in the ministry of Ugandan evangelist Robert Kayanja.[19]

American coverage of Christians in other lands tended overwhelmingly to be positive, despite much reporting on dangerous circumstances. Occasionally, however, the periodicals drew attention to serious difficulties. In 1975, Carl Henry explained in *Christianity Today* how the church in South Korea was trying both to critique the government for its injustices and to maintain the religious liberty that they had enjoyed to advance the gospel.[20] During the years when the Chinese communist government actively suppressed the churches, there was sometimes harsh criticism for local believers who bowed to

---

[16]"British Couple Uses the Gospel to Fight AIDS in Uganda," *Charisma and Christian Life*, January 2000, 18-38; C. Hope Flinchbaugh, "Floods of Love in Mozambique," *Charisma and Christian Life*, June 2000, 72-86.

[17]Ernest Gordon, "From the Missionary Watch Tower," *Sunday School Times*, October 17, 1925, 652.

[18]Aniol Stephen, "The Church at the Top of the World," *Christianity Today*, April 3, 2000, 56-59.

[19]"People and Events," *Charisma and Christian Life*, March 2000, 28-49.

[20]Carl F. H. Henry, "South Korea in the Balances," *Christianity Today*, July 4, 1975, 65-66.

governmental pressure. The *Sunday School Times* in 1950, for instance, did not waver on this issue when it likened churches that cooperated with the Chinese government to those that belonged to the Federal Council of Churches, which naturally the *Sunday School Times* did not approve.[21]

As the century wore on, American periodicals could sometimes pose their judgments with greater reserve. Thus, in 1975 when the churches of Chad were facing the question of how to treat their members who had undergone an anti-Christian initiation ceremony at the insistence of a hostile government, *Christianity Today* recruited an African to offer a measured assessment. Byang H. Kato of the Association of Evangelicals of Africa and Madagascar spoke carefully about the difficulty:

> There is great potential for the churches in Chad now, but presently they are faced with the problem with what to do with members who underwent initiation. In one church all but the pastor and an elder succumbed to [former president] Tombalbaye's threats; in other churches the pastors underwent initiation, but many members resisted—some paying with their lives. One pastor told me how he had been severely beaten and forced to eat human excrement. Some Christian initiates have repented, but the process of healing in the churches will be a long one.[22]

For countries closed to Western missionaries, editors pieced together what information they could about unregistered churches. In 1975 the status of such churches in communist countries was a popular subject in *Christianity Today*, which provided reports on believers in Russia, North Vietnam and China. For these stories, the editors relied on personal accounts, the publications of human rights groups and interviews with expatriates. As an example, the article on North Vietnam was written by a Japanese Christian journalist who had been allowed to visit a show church and to speak with the pastor, though only because he was also willing to listen to a great deal of communist propaganda.[23] Similar reports also appeared in other magazines on communities of

---

[21]Ernest Gordon, "Communism and the Church in China," *Sunday School Times*, November 18, 1950, 981.
[22]"News," *Christianity Today*, June 6, 1975, 99.
[23]"News," *Christianity Today*, April 11, 1975, 31.

believers in North Africa and the Middle East.[24]

Reporting on churches abroad also regularly matched reporting on the churches in North America. Perhaps the most common complaint voiced by both missionaries and leaders at home was the lack of Christian maturity that made it impossible to distinguish believers from their nonbelieving neighbors. In early 2000, a *Christianity Today* correspondent quoted a Romanian Baptist leader as saying, "In my country evangelical Christians are not very distinguishable from the rest of the population in promoting high ethical values"—but then the article went on to say that these words applied just as much in the United States as in Romania.[25] Similarly, *Charisma* pointed out that a story about the divorce of a well-known South African Christian couple in ministry all too sadly paralleled a common American situation.[26]

Surprisingly, the American magazines only rarely reported on what it was like actually to go to church in other parts of the world. By late in the century some coverage was beginning to appear, often by way of commenting on the profusion of worship styles that had developed in the United States. In 1975 *Moody Monthly* included a report that praised the worship services of Greek evangelicals as "simple and predictable," but, "not superficial."[27] In 2000, as part of its report on the new Christian believers in Nepal, *Christianity Today* included a rare report on an actual service:

> Saluting each other with folded hands and saying "Jai Masih" (the Nepalese expression for "Praise the Lord"), they take off their shoes making way inside to squat on a carpeted floor just before 10:30 a.m. Except for a handful of expatriates, the Nepalese Isai Mandali (Gyaneshwor) Church is filled with first-generation Nepali Christians who have braved social and religious constraints to follow Jesus Christ. Every square inch of space is taken and those who are late reluctantly sit outside. At the first strain of a Nepali song, all 2,000 hands, young

[24]Barbara Baker, "Where the Gospel Is a Secret," *Charisma and Christian Life*, January 2000, 42-49.
[25]"The world is much with us" (Letters), *Christianity Today*, February 7, 2000, 17.
[26]"Ray and Lyndie McCauley's Divorce Shakes Churches in South Africa," *Charisma and Christian Life*, October 2000, 46.
[27]Edward Kuhlman, "A Grecian Odyssey," *Moody Monthly*, November 1975, 63-66.

and old, lift in praise to God. This amazing sight brings tears to my eyes. Ten years ago an open meeting of this nature would have been impossible.[28]

Also in 2000, *Charisma* correspondent David Aikman offered an extensive comparison of worship in two Southeast Asian congregations. One was an Anglican charismatic church in Thailand led by a Chinese pastor, the other a house church in mainland China where five hundred Christians crammed into a three story apartment building to attend worship that featured an eighty-minute sermon. In Aikman's words the latter meeting "could not have been less charismatic if it tried." Aikman's point was that each of these services represented an equally valid expression of worship in the body of Christ.[29]

By the year 2000, reports about missionaries who were sent out from churches not in North America and Europe were becoming more common. Of these the most dramatic featured accounts of Africans coming to the United States. One report, which was titled "Intercontinental Ballistic Bishops" told of the actions of Archbishop Moses Tay of Southeast Asia and Archbishop Emannuel Kolini of Rwanda to consecrate two Americans as Anglican bishops so that they might offer an alternative in orthodox teaching and practice to what was otherwise on offer from the American Episcopal Church. Predictably, the presiding bishops of the United States and Canada were not pleased; according to Canada's presiding Episcopal bishops, Michael Peers, "Bishops are not Intercontinental Ballistic Missiles manufactured on one continent and fired into another as an act of aggression."[30] The editors of *Christianity Today* provided no explicit rebuttal, but seemed to suggest that it was a good experience for North Americans to be on the receiving end of missionary labors.

For the most part, the American magazines did not look elsewhere for theological instruction. Throughout the century Europe was clearly

---

[28]Aniol Stephen, "The Church at the Top of the World," *Christianity Today*, April 3, 2000, 56-59.
[29]David Aikman, "Different Churches, Same Spirit," *Charisma and Christian Life*, January 2000, 86.
[30]"World Report," *Christianity Today*, May 22, 2000, 30.

on the theological map, though often only to criticize erring trends. Early on there were similar complaints about the incursions of theological modernism into seminaries and Christian universities in Asia. By 1975, some awareness of theological contributitons from abroad was also becoming visible. Thus, in 1975 *Christianity Today* published an assessment of theologians in India who were responding to appeals for indigenized Christian thinking. The article did not approve of Ramond Panikkar who wanted more dialogue with Hindus because "He [Christ] is the light that illuminates every human being coming into the world. Hence Christ is already there in Hinduism in so far as Hinduism is a true religion. . . . That Christ which is already in Hinduism has not yet unveiled his whole face, has not yet completed his work there." But the magazine did approve of Paul Sudhakar, a converted Hindu, who proclaimed "Christ as the fulfillment of the spiritual aspirations of the Hindu worshiper—i.e., Christ is the Ultimate answer to Hinduism."[31] In other articles that year, Carl Henry wrote essays critiquing liberation theology and probing the theological ideas of Chinese Christian Leader Watchman Nee, while René De Visme Williamson authored an even longer inquiry into liberation theology.[32] In 2000, *Christianity Today* published an African-oriented exposition of the Twenty-Third Psalm.[33] Attention to theological debate had been one of *Christianity Today*'s goals since its founding, but only toward the close of the century did the magazine begin to treat non-Western believers as contributors to theological construction.

Gradually, the dramatic expansion of Christianity in other parts of the world was beginning to work an effect on the periodicals. To be sure, even in the year 2000 most of the attention still focused on the States. But doors and windows were opening ever wider to the winds of change.

---

[31]Bruce Demarest, "Crises and Cross in India," *Christianity Today*, January 3, 1975, 331-32.

[32]Carl F. H. Henry, "What Is Evangelical Liberation," *Christianity Today*, February 14, 1975, 476-78; Henry, "Sharper Focus on Watchman Nee," *Christianity Today*, May 11, 1975, p. 799; René De Visme Williamson "The Theology of Liberation," *Christianity Today*, August 8, 1975, 7-13.

[33]Hannah W. Kinoti, "In the Valley of the Shadow of Idi Amin," *Christianity Today*, June 12, 2000, 78-81.

FRAMEWORKS

Throughout the twentieth century American evangelical periodicals provided their readers with considerable information about the world-wide situation of the Christian faith. In virtually every issue of every magazine there was material about Christian organizations, agencies, churches and individuals beyond the borders of the United States. No other theme, with the exception of general spiritual guidance, was more prominent in the magazines. And the interest in the world was broad—the Moody publications mentioned at least ninety different countries in the five years surveyed here, and in 1950 alone *Moody Monthly* wrote about Christian developments in fifty-four different nations.

At the same time, most of the treatment about other parts of the world was relatively superficial. With some exceptions, reports treated only the surface. Feature stories, up to several pages long, sometimes were able to provide a little depth on the cultural contexts for Christian developments. But most often—for feature stories and the news items, correspondence and editorials—coverage was rapid, fragmentary and disjointed. Typically, treatment of the world offered a paragraph or two of information, a brief barrage of statistics, a testimony, or a brief account of an unusual occurrence. Readers might learn there was persecution in northern India, a new church in Guatemala, clashes with governmental officials in China, an unusual crowd for revival meetings in Nigeria or missionary initiatives in Eastern Europe, but the deep structures supporting these surface events were rarely the focus of attention—that is, the shifting fortunes of tribal loyalties that precipitated persecution, the chances for a new church to flourish, the strategies employed to counteract governmental crackdowns, the persistence over time of converts or the long-term effects of newly opened mission fields.

For the early part of the twentieth century most of the information supplied to American readers came via missionaries, who were in the twofold business of interpreting Christianity (and America) to local nationals but also interpreting the world and national churches to Americans. So long as the missionary view prevailed, evangelism—and often evangelism by itself—was the sum of world Christianity as portrayed in American periodicals. Missionaries naturally tended to write about themselves and their work first and the national churches second. Missionary reports, which in the early part of the century were often published with little editing, were intended to serve many purposes. They described the mission work, created an awareness of the spiritual and physical needs of the mission region, offered a means of accountability to sending constituencies, and communicated the human, financial and spiritual needs of the ministry. Missionaries obviously cared deeply about the people with whom they worked, but the ordinary struggles of ordinary national believers were rarely communicated to American readers, whatever the degree to which missionaries on site understood them. Rather, the central message was conversion.

The magazines surveyed here were, of course, popular magazines aimed at broad audiences, so it would be unfair to expect them to have offered detailed, scholarly accounts of the world situation (or of anything else, for that matter). The magazines did make some use of technical and professional literature, most notably in early years from the solid material found in the *Missionary Review of the World*. So long as this exemplary and very substantial periodical was still around (it was published from 1878 to 1939), editors of the popular magazines enjoyed a rich resource for in-depth coverage of missionaries and world Christianity.[34] Compared to the popular periodicals, the *Missionary Review* delivered much more material on national Christians, even though its main focus remained on the missionaries. The popular magazines made frequent use of the *Missionary Review*, for example in 1925 when a July story on Russian evangelicals in the *Review* was echoed in a November story in the *Sunday School Times* on the same subject. The magazines also borrowed from each other for their world coverage. Ernest Gordon, the long-time columnist in the *Sunday School Times* who wrote regularly on world affairs, gleaned material from the *Missionary Review* and his own wide circle of correspondents. In turn, *Moody Monthly* and the *Pentecostal Evangel* regularly clipped stories from Gordon's column.

---

[34]For an outstanding study of the efforts made to raise world consciousness by A. T. Pierson, who edited the *Review* from 1888 through 1911, see Dana Lee Robert, *Occupy Until I Come: A. T. Pierson and the Evangelization of the World* (Grand Rapids: Eerdmans, 2003).

Later in the century the *International Bulletin of Missionary Research* (published from 1977) again provided a professional journal of high scholarly standards that the popular magazines could mine for their own purposes. By later in the century, editors were also exploiting a much wider array of news services, television and radio reports, and eventually the internet in their search for news. The result was that, though the *International Bulletin* approximated the *Missionary Review* in its thorough coverage and depth of insight, it was probably used less by the popular magazines than its predecessor had been.

Another significant change in the course of the century took place in the nature of the periodicals themselves. By 2000 all of the magazines surveyed were more market driven than their predecessors; all featured less systematic Bible content and straightforward theological writing; all followed more closely the advertising conventions of national media. *Moody Monthly* in 1925 and 1950, and even more the *Sunday School Times* in those two years, published more words over the course of twelve months than did *Christianity Today* in 2000, which at that latter year was by far the most in-depth magazine in the survey. Compared to popular American magazines more generally in 2000, the evangelical ones were still substantial. But compared to evangelical periodicals of earlier years, they made fewer intellectual demands. "Responsible sensationalism" or "celebrity-driven sanctity" might describe the picture by 2000. Earlier, phrases like "intensely and other-worldly pious" or "single-mindedly spiritual" would have been more appropriate. Later issue years appeared more realistic about the Christian life, but less ardent; earlier issue years seemed less realistic, but more devout.

CONCLUSIONS

Over the twentieth century as a whole, the largest change concerned the place of missionaries in brokering information about world Christianity to American readers. By 1950 missionary reports were beginning to give way to more secular sources of international information. The Second World War and then the Cold War altered much more than just politics. These high-visibility phenomena also exerted a great influence on the religious perceptions of Americans. The picture of international conflict between the West and Communism set a pattern for American treatment of the world church. Evangelism remained a focus, but to it was added persecution as a central motif for understanding world Christianity. Not too many years after world events drew attention to large-scale moral conflict, America's own culture wars further heightened motifs of conflict.

Judgments about the general nature of world coverage by the evangelical periodicals must remain impressionistic, but careful reading for five years spaced over the course of the century point toward the following judgments:

- During the first half of the century, the dominant missionary voice probably obscured how much the most important worldwide Christian developments were being driven by local believers acting in accord with their own local agendas.

- During the second half of the century the drama of persecution (first by communists, then by Muslims and Hindus) became a much more dominant theme. This trend certainly reflected developments that were actually taking place, but the suspicion lingers that American press coverage gravitated more readily to instances of conflict than to other important matters like the formation of institutions, the continued advance of evangelism among rural and urban poor, and the indigenization of Christian values in local cultures.

- Significantly, evangelical identification of the Roman Catholic Church as an agent of persecution declined greatly over the course of the century. (Earlier there had been some ambiguity, with Catholicism pictured as oppressive in Latin America, Quebec and Southern Europe, but also occasionally portrayed as itself the object of oppression.)

- For the whole of the century, while some American attention was devoted to the grinding poverty that much of the newer Christian world endured, this feature of world Christianity received far less attention than its prevalence deserved.

In general, judgments can be mixed about how well the evangelical periodicals did in treating the course of world Christianity during the

twentieth century. Negatively considered, the magazines never decisively communicated the magnitude of dramatic change in the twentieth-
century history of Christianity that has been documented elsewhere in
this book. A cynic could say that, from the point of view of the magazines, Western missionaries were always experiencing great successes
around the world, but the worldwide church remained small. Or if
there were places where Christian churches flourished, they had little
in depth to offer American believers. From the magazines one could
hardly guess that Christians elsewhere wrestled seriously with theology, often fell out in angry disputes with each other, regularly ignored
the advice of missionaries, and dealt with a range of spiritual and physical challenges beyond the imagination of many American believers.

Put positively, however, much more can be said. In a country where
the national and local media in general do a poor job of providing reliable information about the world, the evangelical magazines were no
worse—and often much better—than their peers. Although missionary
perspectives long dominated the consideration of world Christianity,
missionaries were (by comparison with all other groups of expatriates)
more concerned for nationals, more interested in their temporal and
eternal wellbeing and more informed about local situations. Much can
be criticized in how the missionaries viewed the world, but missionaries
excelled in much as well. Later in the century when other perceptions
advanced—especially concern for persecution—sensationalism certainly took precedence over a concern for day-to-day life. But the sensationalism was almost never fabricated; the events were really taking
place and did deserve serious spiritual, as well as political, attention.

Finally, whatever flaws attended the efforts of these magazines, they
did keep alive an awareness of the universal communion of saints. Even
with all deficiencies considered, it was still a great advantage for readers
of the *Free Methodist* in 1900 to learn why José Guzman of Santo Do-
mingo was grateful to Methodist missionaries who had brought the
light of the gospel to his family;[35] it was edifying in the best way for
readers of the *Sunday School Times* in 1925 to learn of a Brazilian who,

---

[35]"Missions," *Free Methodist*, February 27, 1900, 10-11.

after his conversion, had read through the Bible, alternatively in English and Portuguese, seventy-five times;[36] it was instructive for readers of *Moody Monthly* in 1950 to sound out the names of many Koreans who were gathering huge numbers of youths for Christian instruction and positive group activities;[37] it provided more insight than available through the three national television networks for readers of the *Pentecostal Evangel* in 1975 to find out how the recent coup in Portugal was opening up opportunities for freer proclamation of the gospel;[38] and it provided the right kind of sobering challenge for readers of *Christianity Today* in 2000 to study an in-depth account of the AIDS crisis in Africa and what Christian leaders—whose names and stories predominated over the names and stories of missionaries—were attempting in response to the crisis.[39] Even if the vision of these periodicals was limited in all sorts of ways, the Big Story in fact was getting through.

---

[36]Y. P. Ribeiro, "Down from the Amazon Valley," *Sunday School Times*, January 17, 1925, 35.

[37]Eleanor Soltau, "Spotlight on Koreans," *Moody Monthly*, November 1950, 213, 216.

[38]Sam Johnson, "City of Flags and Freedom," *Pentecostal Evangel*, March 23, 1975, 8.

[39]Timothy Morgan, "Have We Become Too Busy With Death?" *Christianity Today*, February 7, 2000, 36-44.

9

What Korean Believers Can Learn from American Evangelical History

THE QUESTION OF WHAT KOREAN CHRISTIAN BELIEVERS might learn from the experience of American evangelical Protestants is an especially pertinent one because of the many remarkable similarities that exist between the history of Protestant churches in Korea and the history of Protestant churches in the United States of America.[1] This chapter begins by noting seven of these similarities before going on to describe ways in which Protestant history in Korea has differed from

[1]For some of the material in this chapter, I am grateful to Wheaton College students Vernon Blake Killingsworth, "The Impact of Christian Mission and Bible Translation on the National Spirit of Korea, 1884-1919" (master's thesis, Wheaton College Graduate School, 2001); and Madison Trammel, "The Effect of the Nevius Methods and the Hangul Translation on Korean Christianity" (course paper, Wheaton College Graduate School, 2003). Over the years my friend Prof. Steven Soo-Chan Kang has been an excellent personal tutor for the history of Christianity in Korea. I also much appreciate what I learned from Dr. Yang-Ho Lee, Dr. Paul Junggap Huh and my other exceedingly helpful hosts at Yonsei University's United Graduate School of Theology in October 2004.

Protestant history in the United States. The end of the chapter considers several lessons that Korean believers may be able to draw as they contemplate developments in American Protestant history.

Because of the manifest similarities between Korean and American Christian life, the histories of these two countries have much to offer each other. As those histories unfolded, they revealed the force of direct American influence, but they also illustrated the way that common circumstances can lead to common expressions of the faith.

INITIAL COMPARISONS

The many evangelical and Protestant movements in North America are mostly descended from the early Protestants of England, Scotland and Ireland, especially as given shape by the Puritans who came to the American colonies in the seventeenth century. Puritans emphasized a religion of the Bible and of Christian experience; those emphases have remained strong in the centuries since. Evangelical Protestant churches were the largest and most dominant churches in the United States throughout the nineteenth century. On the eve of the American Civil War in 1860, perhaps as much as one-half of the national population was associated in some way with Methodist, Baptist, Presbyterian, Episcopal or other evangelical churches, and adherents to these evangelical churches made up about three-quarters of all religious adherents. The preeminence of evangelical Protestantism gradually faded after the Civil War, but of course remains a strong presence in the United States.

Modern American evangelicals stress the need for religious conversion ("the new birth"). They hold a high view of the Bible's authority. They value contemporary relevance over religious traditions. And they feature the person of Christ, especially his saving death on the cross. The most visible evangelicals since the Second World War have been leaders of voluntary (or parachurch) agencies like the college ministries InterVarsity Christian Fellowship and Campus Crusade for Christ, the relief agency World Vision, publishing companies like Christianity Today, Inc., radio-driven conglomerates like Focus on the Family, and educational institutions like Moody Bible Institute. Among the best-known evangelical figures are the evangelist Billy Graham, the psychologist and broadcaster James Dobson, the politician and broadcaster Pat Robertson, and Charles Colson, the one-time White House assistant to Richard Nixon, who now heads a Christian ministry to prisons.

In the United States today about one-fourth of the population is associated with theologically orthodox denominations like the Southern Baptist Convention, the Assemblies of God, the Church of the Nazarene, the Baptist Bible Fellowship International, the Presbyterian Church in America, the Churches of Christ and many other smaller evangelical groups. Increasingly, recent immigrants to America make up an ever-larger segment of the adherents to these evangelical churches. About another 10 percent of the population are adherents to African American Protestant churches like the Church of God in Christ, the National Baptist Convention, USA, Inc., the National Baptist Convention, Inc., and the African Methodist Episcopal Church—where many religious beliefs and practices (but not political attitudes) are similar to those of other evangelicals. In addition, significant numbers in denominations that are not as a whole evangelical also maintain traditionally evangelical beliefs concerning salvation in Christ, trust in the Bible and the need to encourage non-Christians to become Christians—that is, more than half in older mainline Protestant churches (Presbyterians, Episcopalians, Lutherans, Methodists) and also many of America's Roman Catholics. Whether defined by beliefs and practices or identification with conservative Protestant denominations, evangelicals are strongest in the American South, and they are weakest in New England and the American Far West. But throughout the country they remain a major presence.

The demography of Protestant adherence in Korea is not the same as in the United States, but it is still impressive in its own right. According to the 2001 edition of *Operation World,* about one-third of South Korea's nearly 47 million people are affiliated with Christian churches. An even higher proportion of these affiliated Christians are members of Protestant churches than in the United States. The denominational mixture is likewise not exactly the same. Yet the presence of Assemblies of God and other Pentecostals, Presbyterians, Methodists, Holiness, Baptist and independent churches makes the Korean ecclesiastical landscape look at least relatively familiar to an American observer.

SIMILARITIES BETWEEN KOREAN AND AMERICAN PROTESTANT HISTORY

Similarities between American Protestant history and Korean Protestant history are striking. In the first instance, Protestant history in both countries shows the advantage when churches are able to take responsibility for directing their own affairs. In the United States, this push to autonomy came about as a consequence of the American Revolution. In 1776 the United States declared their independence from Britain. By 1789, American Methodists, American Episcopalians, American Presbyterians and several other smaller denominations had organized their own independent churches. From that time, many American denominations have sustained helpful relationships with churches outside of the United States, but American Protestants have had the privilege and the responsibility of determining their own destiny.

In Korea, the timing and circumstances were different, but the end result was the same. Unlike the Western missionaries who came to other lands in the nineteenth century, missionaries to Korea emphasized the need for Korean believers to manage their own affairs. In 1890, Dr. John L. Nevius visited Korea and lectured on the same principles that he had tried to implement elsewhere in Asia. Churches, according to Nevius, should be self-supporting, self-propagating and self-governing. He was preaching to a receptive audience. Within a decade of Nevius's visit, Korean-led churches were themselves taking responsibility for fundraising, outreach and governance. As early as 1897, the Presbyterian church in Seoul, which was already directed by Koreans, was sending out members every Sunday for evangelism and supporting that work with its own funds, and it had opened a mission in Haengju. In that same year, churches in Sorai and Pyongyang joined with the Seoul congregation to send funds to India for the relief of people suffering from famine. Missionaries continued to play an active role in Korean church life for many decades thereafter, but much earlier than in other parts of the world Christianity in Korea experienced the transition from missionary direction to indigenous direction.

The statesman and one-time president of Yonsei University, Dr. L. George Paik, once summarized the effect of this indigenization on the Korean situation as it had developed as early as 1910:

> Self-support was successfully carried out. Both self-propagation and self-government were the logical consequences of the self-support program. The persistence of the principle gave the Koreans the feeling that the whole enterprise was theirs. The teachers who taught them were their own servants and the churches in which they worshiped were theirs. . . . It is the self-support principle that created the self-respect, self-reliance and independent spirit which are necessary for any successful movement, and that made the Korean Church active and endowed it with resources which sustained it through all its trials.[2]

A second similarity between Protestant experience in Korea and the United States reflects another dimension of this indigenous reality. In both cases, the churches were part of a process by which local organizations survived or resisted the imposition of imperial force. For the United States, the imperial force was Britain, the mother country, which sought in the eighteenth and early nineteenth century to direct the activities of the Americans in accord with its own wishes. Observers at the time, and historians studying the movement of American independence, have both commented upon the prominent place that "the black regiment" (that is, the clergy dressed in black gowns) occupied in mobilizing spiritual resistance to foreign domination.

For Korea, Japanese imperial forces from 1910 to 1945 attempted much more actively to exert a dominant force in Korean national life. But in both cases, because the churches had already become centers of local organization and local activity, the churches played important roles in resisting the demoralizing force of imperial control. Even someone coming freshly to Korean history cannot help but be struck by the prominence of Christian believers in the March First Movement of 1919. At a time when only a tiny percentage of Koreas were adherents

---

[2]L. George Paik, *The History of Protestant Missions in Korea* (1929; reprint, Seoul: Yonsei University Press, 1970), 422.

of Christian churches, about half of the thirty-three signers of the March First declaration were believers. In Korea the moral force of Christianity was aligned against imperialism even more strongly than it had been in the United States.

A third similarity between the Christian history of Korea and the United States concerns the Bible. In both cases, the Scriptures in native idiom exerted a life-transforming effect on individual Christians, within many denominations and for the country as a whole. In the United States it was a matter of Americans taking as their own the King James Version of the Bible that they inherited from their British ancestors. Although the English language of this translation was familiar, it nonetheless took much dedicated effort to print, promote and distribute the Scriptures before the Bible became nearly omnipresent in American life. A sign of how thoroughly the Bible had become integrated into American culture was provided by the public activities of Abraham Lincoln, sixteenth president of the United States. Lincoln was never a church member, and he always retained some doubts about at least some aspects of orthodox Christian faith. Yet he was a lifelong reader of Scripture. As president during the trauma of America's Civil War, 1861-1865, Lincoln often referred to the Scriptures as providing guidance for his own actions, he called the Bible "the best gift God has given to man," and in his memorable Second Inaugural Address of 1865 he quoted the Bible strategically to make the major points of that unforgettable speech. Since the time of Lincoln, knowledge of Scripture has faded somewhat in American life, but it still exerts a strong residual presence—but only because in its early history the Bible had become an indispensable part of American indigenous Christianity.

In Korea the importance of a Bible translated into the local language and appropriated in the life of the churches is even more evident. Especially important, as we have noted above, was the translation of the Bible into the ordinary Korean language, Hangul, and then the effects that the Hangul Bible had in aiding the spread of Protestant Christianity. In commenting on this significant development, Jeong Man Choi wrote in his dissertation from Fuller Theological Seminary on Bible translation in Korea, "If we fail in the first step of indigenization, i.e.

linguistic indigenization, the other steps of indigenization will never be successful."[3] When the Hangul New Testament—which used the common Korean word for God, *Hananim*—appeared in 1907, it marked an important stage in the indigenization of Scripture for the Korean context. But of course the translation did not become widely used on its own. Rather, it was the dedicated distribution of this translation through the work of Korean pastors, Korean cell group leaders and above all Korean Bible colporteurs that made the Hangul Scriptures into a great engine of spiritual renewal and then of social and cultural transformation. In sum, the strength that American Protestants had drawn from a familiar and beloved translation of the Scriptures was matched, and even exceeded, by the strength that Koreans drew from the Bible translated into Hangul and then aggressively distributed, patiently studied, ardently believed and courageously lived.

A fourth similarity between Protestant experience in the United States and Korea concerns identification with modernizing trends. The history of Christianity in the early United States was distinctive because of how its theologically conservative believers used socially liberal means to advance their cause. When the Frenchman Alexis de Tocqueville visited the United States in the 1830s, he was struck by how vibrant church life was, but also by how free American church life seemed in comparison with the conservatism that prevailed in the churches of Europe. In his landmark study *Democracy in America,* which we have cited before, he therefore wrote words worth comparing to Korea's religious environment: according to de Tocqueville, the American character seemed to be compounded of what he called "two perfectly distinct elements that elsewhere have often made war with each other, but which, in America, they have succeeded in incorporating somehow into another and combining marvelously. I mean to speak of the spirit of religion and the spirit of freedom."[4] Since the time of de Tocqueville, American Christianity has continued to exhibit a striking

---

[3]Jeong Man Choi, "Historical Development of the Indigenization Movement within the Korean Protestant Church with Special Reference to Bible Translation" (D.Miss. diss., Fuller Theological Seminary, 1985), 272.

[4]Alexis de Tocqueville, *Democracy in America*, ed. and trans. Harvey Claflin Mansfield and Delba Winthrop (Chicago: University of Chicago Press, 2000), 43.

degree of modernity. It takes free choice for granted, it is comfortable with open market competition, it is adept at using popular media and popular entertainment for religious purposes, and it is inescapably democratic. In Europe, these features of modern life are usually associated with skepticism or even anti-Christian activity. But in the United States these markers of modernity have all been embraced by many of the churches.

In Korea the situation is similar. Christianity has grown most rapidly among Koreans who are most willing to question old ways and reach towards the new. Joel Carpenter of Calvin College has studied the relationship of Korean churches in the United States and the situation for the churches in Korea. His conclusion as to why the proportion of Christian believers is higher among Korean Americans than in Korea itself has to do with the acceptance by Korean believers of certain aspects of modern life. Christianity in Korea, to put it in Carpenter's words, grew more rapidly among "mobile, cosmopolitan, urbanized middle-class people than [among] their more traditional countrymen." In Korea from the 1870s and 1880s, Christianity was presented as "something new and modern." In turn, Koreans accepted it "as a means to the modern, cosmopolitan way of life."[5] In this linking of Christianity with an openness to urban life, economic growth, democracy and modern communications, Korean Protestants have replicated the experience of their American Protestant counterparts.

Yet a fifth similarity between American and Korean histories is the large role played by warfare in defining the character of Protestant values in both countries. A substantial part of my own work as a historian has been devoted to showing how American Protestant Christianity was shaped by the ideologies embraced in the American Revolution of the 1770s and then contested in the Civil War of the 1860s. The pathbreaking work of George Marsden has similarly shown how much the experience of World War I determined the character of the great fundamentalist-modernist struggles of the 1920s.[6] In more recent history,

[5]Joel Carpenter, "Korean Christianity and the American Religious Experience" (presentation to the Asian Bilingual Program, Haggard School of Theology, Los Angeles, 2001), 6.
[6]Mark A. Noll, *Christians in the American Revolution* (Grand Rapids: Eerdmans, 1976); Noll,

a key ingredient in defining the character of Protestant churches in the United States has been their stance, for or against, the Vietnam War of the 1960s and 70s and, in the early twenty-first century, an ongoing Iraq War.

The details are not the same, but the impact of warfare on the churches of the Korean Peninsula has been even larger than in the United States. Military occupation followed by the Second World War and then followed by the great destruction of the Korean War provided the background against which the churches of Korea did their work. It is in fact possible to interpret the period leading up to the Korean War and then the war itself as critically important for the recent Christian history of the Korean nation. The migration of Christian believers from North to South, the emergence of leaders who would become key figures in guiding the church growth of the 1960s and following years, the positive image of Christian faith communicated through the Western relief agencies active in Korea during and after the war, the loosening of missionary control over church life and theological education, and the endurance of native Korean institutions through the traumas of conflict and the struggles of rebuilding—all of these factors made the Korean War a very important event for the church history of Korea. Survival and advance through the perils of war is yet another way that Korean church life has resembled church life in the United States.

A sixth similarity between the histories of Christianity in the two countries is the prominence of revival as a vehicle for strengthening the Protestant churches. It is an exaggeration to say that American Christianity is built on a foundation of revivalism, but not too much of an exaggeration. The colonial Great Awakening of the mid-eighteenth century, in which George Whitefield was the itinerating spark and Jonathan Edwards was the careful theological apologist, began the modern history of American evangelicalism. Intensive efforts by great numbers of Methodists itinerants fanned the feeble coals of living Christianity in the early decades of the United States' national history.

America's God: From Jonathan Edwards to Abraham Lincoln (New York: Oxford University Press, 2002); George Marsden, *Fundamentalism and American Culture* (New York: Oxford University Press, 1980).

For nearly two hundred years the best-known public figures in American Protestantism have been revivalists like Charles G. Finney, Dwight L. Moody and Billy Graham. Most American Christians have not had first-hand contact with such well-known revivalists, but all are familiar with the revival style. That style emphasizes the born-again experience, it works hard at mobilizing individuals for concentrated campaigns, it insists upon immediate solutions to combat the effects of sin, it calls upon people for all-out dedication to the cause of Christ. As a style, even more than as a phenomenon, revivalism has decisively shaped the experience of American churches.

And so it has been in Korea as well. The great Pyongyang revivals of 1903 and 1907 were significant for all of world Christian history, as well as for the history of Christianity in Korea. To Korea these revivals bequeathed a great confidence in the active power of God. They also bequeathed specific practices—like unison prayer, early morning prayer and overnight prayer—that have helped to define the character of Korean Protestantism since those early days. For the world at large, these early revivals coming out of Pyungyang were also important for showing that at least some aspects of Western revival traditions could be re-formed in non-Western settings for the causes of conversion, church growth and the expansion of Christian influence. Thus, in the early years of the twenty-first century, as Protestants around the world study the events of one hundred years ago for what they may teach about Christian possibilities today, eyes are drawn to Korea as well as to the Welsh revivals of 1904-1905 and the Azusa Street revival of 1906 in Los Angeles. The particular importance of the Pyungyang revivals in these commemorations is to remind Westerners that revival is not a gift from the Christian West to the rest of the world, but a gift of God to people wherever in the world and whenever he chooses to bestow it. For Koreans, the revivalistic nature of their faith is yet another bond to the character of American Protestantism where currents of revival have always flowed strongly.

A final similarity between the Protestant histories of the United States and Korea concerns missionary motivation. During the nineteenth century Americans believers were much more a missionized people than a missionary people. In 1800, with the exception of a few struggling ventures among Native American Indians, there were no American Protestants engaged in missionary service. As we have already seen, a century later in 1900 there were around four thousand or about one-fourth of the world's total Protestant missionary force. By the mid-1970s there were about fifty thousand American Protestant missionaries, or about two-thirds of all the Protestant missionaries in the world. Since that time, the absolute number of American missionaries has leveled off, and the proportion of the world total has declined. The main point revealed by these numbers is the great missionary interest that, after the early years of their development, could be seen among American evangelical Protestants. That interest reflected a combination of factors—increased commitment to evangelization, increased financial resources at the disposal of missionary-minded believers, increased awareness of the world through education and increased American engagement with the world through trade.

The same combination of factors has also been at work among Korean Protestants over the course of the last century. In 1900 there were few, if any, Koreans active in crosscultural missionary service. According to an informative article published recently by Steve S. C. Moon, in 2000 there were at least 8,100 Korean Protestants active in crosscultural missionary service, with the number growing by at least 1,000 each year.[7] A survey in 2007 by David Barrett and his colleagues counted more than 15,000.[8] As in the United States, a concern for missions has been combined with the means and opportunity to engage in missionary service. The proliferation of missionaries from non-Western regions is also being witnessed in other parts of the world, for example, in Brazil, India, Nigeria and elsewhere. But no other non-Western missionary enterprise so clearly resembles the pattern of earlier American history as what has happened in Korea.

---

[7]Steve S. C. Moon, "The Recent Korean Missionary Movement: A Record of Growth, and More Growth Needed," *International Bulletin of Missionary Research* 27, no. 1 (January 2003): 11-16.

[8]David B. Barrett, Todd M. Johnson and Peter F. Crossing, "Missiometrics 2007," *International Bulletin of Missionary Research* 31 (January 2007): 31.

LESSONS

Even a preliminary survey of Korean and American Protestant Christianity shows that there is much to ponder in the two histories. In both places, Protestants have flourished through autonomous development; they have defined themselves against the forces of imperialism; they have been strengthened by an indigenous translation of the Bible; they have embraced modernization along with orthodox Christian faith; they have been deeply affected by the tides of war; they are marked by the effects of revival; and they are deeply committed to the cause of crosscultural missions. Such a striking array of parallels cries out for further analysis.

But, of course, responsible analysis must also recognize the major differences that exist between Protestant experience in Korea and the United States. Christianity has been central in American civilization longer than in Korea. Protestants in Korea have never dominated their national culture the way evangelical Protestants dominated American culture during the middle decades of the nineteenth century. The churches of the United States have never had to endure occupation by a foreign power, and not since the 1860s has warfare at home troubled the ongoing life of the churches. The background of classical Western learning highlighted different problems for Christian response than Korean Christians face in addressing classical Asian learning. Western folk piety, with its persistent recourse to magic, provides different challenges for practical Christian living than Korean believers face in responding to Korean folk piety, with the strong presence of shamanism. The American churches have never known a diaspora such as the Korean churches have experienced over the last fifty years. American churches are probably less informed about conditions in other parts of the world than Korean churches (that is, more American television pumped into Korea than Korean television). These are only some of the historical differences that make for contrasts between Korean Protestants and American Protestants.

Yet despite these and other differences, the parallels remain impressive. The striking quality of these parallels suggests the possibility that Christian evaluation of the history of evangelical Protestants in the

United States may offer points to ponder for Protestants in Korea. If, because of parallels with Korean Protestant history, this assessment of the American scene has something to offer Koreans (and other regions of the newly Christian world), it may be instructive.

Four prominent features of American evangelical experience can be singled out for attention. Each has contributed greatly to the positive influence of Christianity in American society as well as in other parts of the world. But with each strength there are also weaknesses. These are the four prominent features:

- In American history, evangelical Protestantism has shown great strength as an individualistic form of Christianity.
- It has shown great strength as a revivalistic form of Christianity.
- It has shown great strength as a culturally dominant form of Christianity.
- It has shown great strength as a form of Christianity well adapted to American culture.

First, the individualism of American evangelicalism is connected to great energy, dedication and personal sacrifice. Evangelicals in America have stressed, and continue to stress, the need for people to make a personal decision for Christ. They urge their friends and associates individually to experience the new birth. The signature conclusion of rallies held by Billy Graham and countless other evangelists has been to ask individuals to get up out of their seats and come to the front of the hall or auditorium to be counseled individually as they receive Christ. They stress that individuals who come to Christ can personally make a difference in their homes, places of employment and in society as they move out in faith.

This stress on the meaning of the gospel for individuals has over the centuries produced a large harvest. This individualism is the key to much of the energy, much of the dedication, much of the sacrifice that has characterized American Protestant churches when they have been at their best and most effective. The sense that God loves me, that God is ready in Christ and through the power of the Holy Spirit to forgive my sin, that God offers (in the famous words of the Four Spiritual Laws of Campus Crusade for Christ) a wonderful plan for my life— this message has constituted a great stimulus to evangelism, to church formation, to mission and to social action.

But the good harvest of individualistic Christianity also contains some weeds. Outsiders have often looked upon American Protestants as too individualistic, too much driven by personal concerns, too little concerned about communities of faith. This criticism once was prominent among Europeans looking across the Atlantic at events in America. It is now also heard from Asians, Africans and Latin Americans as they gain personal experience of Christianity in America. Such observers have asked if egotism must be the price for personal engagement, if schism must be the result of personal dedication. They have seen American churches torn apart by a seemingly endless list of less-than-overwhelming reasons: personality disputes, ego trips, preferences in music, preferences in sermon length, preferences in politics, economic class, race, denominational pride, eccentric interpretations of a limited part of the Bible, very eccentric interpretations of a limited part of the Bible, and so on. They have also seen American Protestants with little to offer as a Christian response to social and cultural problems that demand more than just the actions of individuals.

As an American evangelical Christian, my own conviction is that there can be no living, vital Christianity where individuals are not renewed in the depths of their own personal beings to love and serve the living God. But it is also easy to recognize that when individualism begins to destroy "the communion of the saints," that stress on what individuals can and should do has gone too far.

Second, American evangelical Christianity is also a religion deeply shaped by a commitment to revivalism. The benefits of a revivalistic heritage are significant. A religion defined by revivalists keeps the question of personal salvation uppermost. It is not prone to write off marginalized races or the poor as unimportant. And it is alert to the power of God. Revivals breathe life into the people of God, and American Protestants have often benefited from the revivalism that has played such a large role in their history.

But with the good of revivalism also come problems. Fixation on revival, for example, can obscure the fact that God is Lord of day-to-day activities as well as of unusual times of spiritual refreshing, that he is lord over the problems of communities as well as the problems of individuals, that he is lord of realms defined by nature as well as of realms experienced by grace.

A different problem with revivalism lies in its anti-traditionalism. Revivals call people to Christ as a way of escaping tradition. They call upon individuals to take the step of faith for themselves. In so doing they often leave the impression that individual believers can accept nothing from others, nothing handed on from the past. Everything of value in the Christian life has to come from the individual's own choice—not just personal faith, but every scrap of wisdom, understanding and conviction about the faith. Revival also becomes a problem when it leads Christian groups to concentrate so hard on results that all else fades into insignificance. Results are important for Christian growth, but they are not the only important thing.

Revival does not necessarily have to be promoted in exactly these forms, but in America it often has been. The form of revivalism that eventually came to influence evangelical church life so strongly was activistic, immediatistic and individualistic. As such, it was able to mobilize great numbers for the cause of Christ. But also as such—with its neglect of day-to-day realities, a scorn for tradition and an overconcentration on countable results—American revivalism has done much to restrict full appropriation of the Christian gospel.

Third, evangelical Christians have also experienced long periods of time when they have been culturally dominant in the United States. The greatest dominance was in the decades before the Civil War. Although that position of dominance has faded, still in several parts of the country evangelicals to this day maintain a strong position. Even over the last century, at least in some regions and on some matters, evangelicals have shaped cultural standards, directly influenced political decisions and set the tone for social interactions.

From positions of strong cultural authority, evangelicals have done much good. They have reinforced traditional morality through the law and through informal means. They have raised a lot of money that was then put to good use for evangelistic and social purposes. They have provided children and students with strong educational resources. These positive accomplishments would have been much harder to achieve if evangelicals had been marginalized in American society.

At the same time, there have been dangers as American evangelicals grew accustomed to the exercise of cultural authority. As an example, it has been difficult for some evangelicals to encounter adversity or to suffer the loss of cultural power. Since so many North American evangelical prayers for success have been answered positively, American evangelicals do not always know how to react when God asks them to pass through the valley of shadow. They too easily assume that the ordinary Christian life is one of prosperity, triumph and success, instead of marginality, poverty and worldly failure. And so they have not been able to realize that one important test of Christian vitality is the ability to trust in God when things go wrong as well as when they go right.

After he had twice visited the United States in the 1930s, Dietrich Bonhoeffer wrote sympathetically and yet critically about what it has meant for American Christians to exert great cultural influence: "The secularization of the church on the continent of Europe arose from the misinterpretation of the reformers' distinction of the two realms; American secularization derives precisely from the imperfect distinction of the kingdoms and offices of church and state, from the enthusiastic claim of the church to universal influence in the world."[9] These words are especially sobering at a time (as at the writing of this book) when American evangelicals are being asked by some of their leaders to become even more active in asserting their political rights in the effort to retain authority in their society.

Finally, American evangelical Christianity has shown remarkable strength in adapting to the shape of American culture. In the world's most advanced economy, evangelicals are adept at presenting the gospel in the marketplace of popular culture. In a society dominated by the

[9]Dietrich Bonhoeffer, "Protestantism Without Reformation," in *No Rusty Swords: Letters, Lectures and Notes from the Collected Works of Dietrich Bonhoeffer*, vol. 1, ed. Edwin H. Robertson, trans. Robertson and John Bowden (New York: Harper & Row, 1965), 108.

practices of science, evangelicals have worked hard at showing the compatibility of Christianity and science. In a liberal and democratic society, evangelicals have shown how the gospel empowers the individual. In sharp contrast to the recent religious history of Western Europe, American evangelicals have continued to make their message heard in a society increasingly defined by the norms of democratic individualism.

In the past, once-large denominations, like the Congregationalists, which relied upon their hereditary leadership of established society, experienced a greatly reduced impact on American life. Those like the Methodists and the Baptists, which exploited innovative revival techniques to carry the gospel to ordinary people, flourished. In the early twenty-first century, churches and Christian movements adjusted to mobility, therapy, consumer tastes and high standards of entertainment do very well. American evangelicals, in other words, have mastered the techniques of American society. They have had long training in speaking the languages of democracy, liberalism and the market. In turn, these abilities have been put to use in keeping Christianity relevant, not (to be sure) for all, but for broad stretches of the American public.

But the degree to which evangelicals have succeeded at being at home in American society specifies also the degree of danger that this situation brings to the Christian faith. From one side, American evangelicals sometimes have had difficulty in telling the difference between beliefs and practices that are treasured because they are Christian and beliefs and practices that are treasured because they are American. For issues ranging from politics and entertainment to music and preaching, it would help American evangelicals to probe carefully the ultimate origin of what they believe and what they do.

From another angle, American evangelicals have also had difficulty in telling the difference between beliefs and practices of general, universal value and beliefs and practices of value in America but not elsewhere. The great missiologist Andrew Walls once provided an illustration of this difficulty when he discussed the commitment of overseas missionaries to American traditions concerning the separation of church and state:

If there is one doctrine characteristic of American Christianity as a whole, distinguishing it from the European stream that in so many respects it continues, it must be that of the separation of church and state. The widespread acceptance of this doctrine was due to a civil rather than a theological proposition, arising from the historic situation of the infant United States. American churches have come to adopt it as an article of faith, and American missions have carried it into a variety of overseas spheres. The effects have been paradoxical. American missions have tended to think of themselves as nonpolitical; how can it be otherwise if church and state live in different spheres. Non-Americans have seen continual political implications in their activities: how can it be otherwise if church and state inhabit the same sphere, or at least overlapping spheres?[10]

Walls is saying that, however appropriate the separation of church and state has been to Americans in America, it is wrong to assume that this local tradition should be assumed to be the only possibility for Christian believers elsewhere in the world. This caution applies to other features of American evangelicalism as well.

*   *   *

The history of Christianity in Korea testifies to the weight of direct American influence. Even more, it shows that within a setting sharing some features in common with the American setting, forms of Christianity similar to American forms have flourished. What Koreans may learn from noting these parallels is primarily for Koreans to decide. What Americans may learn is to give thanks for the progress of the gospel that has taken place within their borders and for whatever can be evaluated as positive in American influence abroad. They may also be encouraged to pause with caution and ask which aspects of Christianity's American indigenization have been most faithful, and which have been least faithful, to the character of Christianity itself.

---

[10]Andrew F. Walls, *The Missionary Movement in Christian History* (Maryknoll, N.Y.: Orbis, 1996), 232.

10

The East African Revival

On Monday, September 22, 1935, a roomful of evangelical leaders gathered for a day of spiritual renewal.[1] They confessed their sins to one another and spent time resolving their differences. They studied biblical texts from their Scofield Reference Bibles, a study version that was the standard for American fundamentalists. They prepared a chart outlining a week of conference topics: Tuesday—Sin, Wednesday—Repentance, Thursday—New Birth, Friday—Separation, Saturday—Holy Spirit and the Victorious Life, Sunday—Testimonies, Monday—Praise Gathering. They sang songs that were popular in American and British evangelical circles, including "Spirit of the Living God, Fall Afresh on Me" and "What Can Wash Away My Sins?" But as an indication that this gathering was not taking place in southern California or at the Keswick campgrounds in the north of England, the song that moved participants the most was sung in Luganda, "Tukutendereza Yesu, Yesu Omwana gw'endiga, . . ." (We praise

---

[1]J. E. Church, *Quest for the Highest: A Diary of the East African Revival* (Devon, U.K.: Paternoster, 1981), 116-25.

you Jesus / Jesus lamb of God / Your blood cleanses me / I praise you, Savior).

The scene was Kabale, Uganda, and the men around the circle were mostly Africans: Yosiya Kinuka, Blasio Kigozi, Simeon Nsibambi, Yusufu Biangwa. Before the end of January, Blasio would be dead of "Relapsing Fever" caused by tick bite, but a young man named William Nagenda would soon take his place and become more influential than all who gathered at the earlier meeting. One white face in the group belonged to Joseph Church, a young medical doctor who had arrived from England seven years before. During his student days at Cambridge University, Church had been strongly affected by the British Keswick movement with its stress on personal holiness, the infilling of the Holy Spirit and the need to offer God the "full surrender" of one's life. He had also taken part in early gatherings of Moral Re-Armament, a young persons' movement overseen by an American, Frank Buchman, that featured weekend spiritual retreats where participants talked about their personal lives in ways that often moved into public confession. By 1935, expressions of Christianity that resembled both Keswick and Moral Re-Armament had arrived in Uganda and surrounding regions. They had been taken up enthusiastically by dedicated Ugandans. The East African Revival was underway. (See map on p. 179.)

The revival would expand geographically and socially from its origins in the late 1920s through the five-country area of Uganda, Rwanda, Burundi, Kenya and Tanzania (formerly the mainland Tanganyika and the island Zanzibar). The revival's permanent legacy is the distinctly evangelical flavor that continues to mark the schools, mission agencies and almost all the churches of these countries. Its influence is felt to the present in the day-to-day lives of millions of ordinary believers throughout this region that is marked by great cultural and economic promise, but also by grinding poverty, devastating disease and recurrent tribal violence. The revival also exerts a considerable effect in the realm of international church connections (independent Protestant, Anglican and even Catholic) because of the prominence that second- and third-generation *balokole* (the "saved ones" of the revival) have attained. Especially noticeable in recent years has been the revival's presence in the

Table 10.1

The Countries Most Affected by the East African Revival

	Kenya[a]	*Tanzania*[b]	*Uganda*[c]	*Rwanda*[d]	*Burundi*[e]
Area	224,000 sm[f]	363,000[g]	92,000[h]	10,100[i]	10,700[j]
Population	30.1m	33.5m	22m	7.7m	6.7m
Languages	61	135	46	1[k]	4
Christian adherents	79%	51%	89%	81%	90%
Catholics	23%	25%	42%	43%	57%
Anglicans	9%	8%	40%	11%	7%
Other Protestants	29%	17%	6%	19%	13%
Independents	23%	2%	3%	1%	2%
Orthodox	2%	--	--	--	--
Muslims	8%	32%	6%	11%	3%
Traditional	12%	15%	4%	4%	7%
Jesus Film[l]	20+16	15+27	19+16	40%	most

[a]Independent from Britain 1963; good economic growth until 1976, and relative stability thereafter; but also ongoing suffering from corruption and "venal elite"; Pres. Moi finessed power (as minority Kipsigis) over Kikuyu, Luo, and Luyia; effects of Revival strongest 1948-1960; 14% of pop. AIDS infected.

[b]Tanganyika independent from Britain in 1961, the island Zanzibar in 1963, united as Tanzania in 1964; early socialism a disaster economically; since 1992 a multi-party democracy; Zanzibar heavily Muslim, former headquarters of Arabic slave trade; relatively peaceful country in recent decades.

[c]Independent from Britain 1962; economic growth (on coffee) into 1972 (Asian business community expelled); Milton Obote in power (N. tribalist) 1967, followed by Idi Amin 1971 (800,000-2m perished in next 8 years); Amin overthrown 1979; Obote returned; continued intertribal conflict, though some improvement; some success vs. AIDS (from 25% of pop. to 10%), but still a major problem.

[d]Independent from Belgium in 1962, hereditary Tutsi rule; Hutu rebellion and genocide in 1994 (about 1 million slain, another million expelled); E. African Revival began here in late 1920s and 1930s.

[e]Independent from Belgium in 1962, same Tutsi-Hutu tensions as in Rwanda; Tutsi in control but massive human rights violations; perpetual strife since 1980s; ethnic strife, Great Lakes War, refugees, etc., make Burundi one of the poorest countries on earth.

[f]Larger than California, smaller than Texas.

[g]About the size of Texas plus New Mexico.

[h]Slightly smaller than Oregon.

[i]About the size of Maryland.

[j]About the size of Maryland.

[k]French and English are also official languages.

[l]Languages in which film is available, or % of population that has seen it.

[Information for this table is from the country reports in Patrick Johnstone and Jason Mandryk, *Operation World: Twenty-First Century Edition* (Waynesboro, Ga.: Authentic Media, 2001).]

worldwide Anglican Communion where a number of influential African bishops have spearheaded efforts to discipline the Episcopal Church in the United States and the Canadian Anglican Church for their approval of same-sex marriage and willingness to ordain gay bishops. Most of these bishops come from the *balokole*.

The East African Revival poses a most interesting set of questions for the issues taken up in this book. It bears unmistakable marks reflecting the influence of British (and American) evangelicalism; its best-known current representatives align closely with Western moral and religious conservatives; and its practices, attitudes and doctrines seem to mirror common features of an American style of religious life. Is the East African Revival only twentieth-century Western evangelicalism transplanted into a new setting? A brief summary of the revival and its prominent characteristics cannot answer such questions completely. Yet it can point to the conclusion that, even with much borrowed from the Christian West and much that imitates some forms of Western Christianity, the East African Revival again illustrates more an American pattern of development rather than an overwhelming American (or Western) influence.

EARLY EAST AFRICAN CHRISTIANITY

The modern history of Christianity in East Africa began in the 1870s when the Church Missionary Society (CMS), an evangelical Anglican agency, and the Catholic White Fathers, led by Cardinal Charles Lavigerie, made preliminary excursions into the Buganda region surrounding Lake Victoria.[2] Soon other Protestant and Catholic missionaries, still mostly from Britain and France, joined them and took up their work at a critical juncture in African history. Three different long-term forces were coming together in East Africa at the same time. First was

---

[2]For the material of this chapter I have drawn on Adrian Hastings, *The Church in Africa, 1450-1950* (New York: Oxford University Press, 1994); John Karanja, *Founding an African Faith: Kikuyu Anglican Christianity, 1900-1945* (Nairobi: Uzima Press, 1999)—my thanks to Paul Heidebrecht for referring me to Karanja's fine book; Kevin Ward, "East Africa," in *A History of Global Anglicanism* (New York: Cambridge University Press, 2006); John Karanja, "Evangelical Attitudes Toward Democracy in Kenya," in *Evangelical Christianity and Democracy in Africa*, ed. Terence O. Ranger (New York: Oxford University Press, 2008), 67-93; and expert papers by Wheaton College students Lindsay Brummer and Samuel Olson.

religious competition; in this case, several Catholic and several Protestant mission bodies jostled with each other (and with Muslims whose history on the African east coast and on the island of Zanzibar extended far back in time) for access to the people of a region being opened to extensive contact with the outside world.

Second was the nature of that outside involvement. Missionaries were in the vanguard, but a far greater pressure was coming from European nations as they began the notorious "scramble for Africa" that in a very short period at the end of the nineteenth century carved up the entire continent into zones of European domination. The drive for African colonies fed Europe's expansive economic aspirations; even more, it exported Europe's intense military and national competitions. After the Congress of Berlin in 1885, when diplomats divided Africa into zones of European control, Western nations moved rapidly to secure "their" colonies and to make them over into productive contributors to worldwide empires. So it was that hard on the heels of the CMS and the White Fathers came colonial officials from Germany (Tanganyika and Zanzibar), Britain (Uganda, Kenya) and Belgium (Rwanda, Burundi) to administer, organize, educate and exploit their new African possessions.

Third were the momentous consequences for traditional African life that resulted from European colonization. Foreign influence was not in itself new; in East Africa that influence had been mainly Arab, but it had been restricted to the coast and to the island of Zanzibar. Now, however, a new type of outside influence was at work. European colonizers wanted to systematize traditional African life along European lines. Thus, a European concept of the nation-state, with broad central control and unified national purpose, was imposed on vast areas of Africa where tribal allegiance and local customs had provided the main principles of human organization. The region's many language groups were collected together into the new colonies of East Africa, which bisected traditional tribal and linguistic homelands (see table 10.1). The result was that ancient cultural, political, economic, social and religious patterns underwent radical change. European conflicts exported to Africa, as when European powers conscripted hundreds of thousands of Africans to work as their military proxies during the First World War, increased the disruption of traditional life. Social order was by no means idyllic in East Africa before the arrival of European colonizers, since tribal warfare, slavery, sometimes inhuman treatment of women, and agricultural inefficiency were all part of traditional life. In addition, the new era of European colonization brought much that East Africans embraced eagerly on their own volition, including especially Western education and, often, Christianity. But when a grid of European power was overlaid upon traditional tribal ways of life, the unsettling conditions were put in place that have defined much of recent African history—including both spectacular instances of personal empowerment, spiritual illumination, economic advance and political self-determination, as well as spectacular upsets, dislocations, social disasters and inflamed tribal conflicts.

The Christian factor in the European scramble for Africa was that European regimes expected their missionaries to assist in the pacification of native populations. Missionaries, as scholars like Lamin Sanneh and Andrew Porter have pointed out, were often far less the simple servants of empire than standard post-colonial accounts now portray them to be.[3] In fact, sometimes they were the lone voices in the early colonial era that denounced exploitation and worked altruistically for the Africans. Yet the Christianity they brought to East Africa was interwoven inextricably with the advance of Empire.

The first chapter in this great encounter was bloody. In the 1880s, before European rule was securely in place and while traditional African rulers maintained control over their territories, missionaries operated beyond the safety net of empire. Self-sacrificing Anglican and Catholic pioneers won converts among especially well-placed younger Bugandans and seemed, briefly, to be winning over Bugandan chiefs as well. But traditional tensions combined with apprehension about European arrivals created instability. Martyrdom—of missionaries, but also many of the most promising first converts—resulted.

From the late 1880s, as colonial rule advanced, threats of persecu-

---

[3]Lamin Sanneh, *Disciples of All Nations: Pillars of World Christianity* (New York: Oxford University Press, 2008), 131-61; Andrew Porter, *Religion Versus Empire? British Protestant Missionaries and Overseas Expansion, 1700-1914* (New York: Manchester University Press, 2004).

tion declined and rates of conversion increased. The East African Revival of the 1930s and following years would be a revival in the strict sense of the word—that is, a movement that brought life back to Christian groups whose practice of faith had grown cold. The Christians it sought to revive emerged by the late nineteenth and early twentieth centuries when Africans accepted the new faith that accompanied the advance of colonial rule. In what would become Uganda, considerable success for the Anglican Church advanced step-by-step with British rule; a parallel situation happened for the Catholic Church in Belgian-colonized Rwanda and Burundi. In Kenya, the advance of both Catholicism and various Protestant denominations was hastened by the determination of Kenyans from many tribes to take advantage of the new educational opportunities provided by the schools that all missions established. In the first decades of the new century the number of Christian adherents grew rapidly in the new European colonies of East Africa.

One of the results of the rapid growth in Christian adherence was tension between traditional African practices and the ways of the missionaries. The most visible of these tensions arose from missionary objections to the ancient practice of female circumcision.[4] When in the 1920s various Western agencies began to call for a reform or cessation of this widespread rite of initiation, many of the newly Christianized Africans agreed and banned the practice in their churches. But others did not agree. The response of the latter was not to abandon Christianity, but to claim sanction for their traditional practice from passages in their newly translated Bibles where circumcision was often mentioned. If, as they read these new Bibles, the practice was biblical, and if the missionaries were perceived as promoting alien Western ideologies, the natural step was to form churches entirely liberated from missionary control. This is, in fact, what happened, especially among the Kikuyu, Embu and Meru in Kenya. The African

---

[4]For this material I am indebted to my Wheaton College student Amy Newhouse, who made good use of Jacob Z. Kibor, "Persistence of Female Circumcision Among the Marakwet of Kenya: A Biblical Response to a Rite of Passage" (Ph.D. diss., Trinity International University, 1998); and Jocelyn Murray, "The Church Missionary Society and the 'Female Circumcision' Issue in Kenya, 1929-1932," *Journal of Religion in Africa* 8 (1976): 92-104.

Independent Pentecostal Church of Africa was the major new denomination formed as a result of this conflict. Its record of independent action began with this division in the 1930s, but then has carried on through later decades as it (unlike churches influenced by the East African Revival) supported the Mau-Mau independence movement of the 1950s and later (again unlike churches of the Revival) backed the corrupt regime of Kenyan president Daniel arap Moi.[5] To this day, adherents of African Independent Churches in Kenya make up a much higher proportion of the Christian population than in the other East African countries (see table 10.1).

So it was that, even before the new Christian churches of East Africa experienced revival, they underwent division over how much and what kind of Western influence to accept. For the revival itself, the key background factors were the general acceptance of Christianity as part of the advance of colonial rule and the thorough disruption of traditional African life entailed by colonization.

A BRIEF SKETCH OF THE EAST AFRICAN REVIVAL

In human terms, the revival that came to these still new African churches sprang from a singular combination of personal teamwork and social adaptability. The teamwork involved first a talented young Ugandan, Simeon Nsibambi, and a missionary doctor, Joseph Church, and then a much-broadened circle of cooperation.[6] The social adaptability concerned the appeal of a particular Christian message at a particular stage of East African history.

Simeon Nsibambi was born in 1897 to the chief of a dominant Ugandan tribe, he received a solid education in British schools, and he served with distinction in the African Native Medical Corps during World War I. His Christian conversion occurred in 1922, shortly after he began work as a health officer in the colonial government. With many of his aspiring peers, Nsibambi took steps toward study-

---

[5]Karanja, "Democracy in Kenya," 73-74.
[6]For the lives of these two leaders, I have relied on Mark Shaw's helpful work on Nsibambi in "A Hunger for Holiness," in the special issue on "The African Apostles," *Christian History* 79 (2003): 28-31; Church, *Quest for the Highest*; and the excellent research of Carolyn Nystrom.

ing abroad, but those steps were frustrated. In his disappointment, Nsibambi was driven to reevaluate his spiritual condition. After a period of doubt and anxiety, he received a vision from God that asked him to compare the ephemeral value of a foreign scholarship with the eternal worth of the Christian gospel he already possessed. The vision transformed Nsibambi into an active lay preacher who frequently addressed the crowds around Kampala's Anglican Cathedral about their need for self-renunciation and a living faith. His plea urged the Christianized population of this new colony to exchange formal religion for true belief.

The meeting that sparked a more organized approach to revival took place with Dr. Joseph Church in 1929. Church was in Kampala on a short visit from his home base in Gahini, Rwanda, where he served as the CMS physician at one of the many stations where the mission was following its standard plan for establishing a school, church and hospital in a single location. Though a busy doctor, Church actively supported the teaching and evangelistic goals of the mission. From the start, however, he was set apart from at least some of his peer missionaries by his reliance on African assistants for these activities. Church's linguistic abilities were good, but his practice from early on was to encourage African hospital helpers to do the preaching and teaching. In this move he was following the lead of an earlier leader of the CMS, Henry Venn, who in the nineteenth century—before the European scramble for Africa shifted missionary strategies—insisted on self-support, self-propagation and self-governance as the goal for missionary churches.

In September 1929, Church was physically and mentally exhausted from two years of intense labor against the ravages of a devastating famine; spiritually, he felt an equal exhaustion that he defined, in terms of his Keswick background, as spiritual emptiness. At this crucial junction, he found himself in Kampala. There just outside the cathedral, as Church later recalled the event, "was a man in a dark suit standing beside his motor bike. He spotted me and ran out to greet me. It was Simeon Nsibambi whom I had met in March. . . . I said that I was looking for a new infilling of the Holy Spirit and the victorious life. He warmed to this as we talked. I had been praying for a long time that God would lead me to one really saved African with whom I could have deep fellowship." Nsibambi and Church spent the weekend together in praying and studying the Scofield Bible. Neither was the same thereafter. Church's autobiographical testimony recorded the transformative character of this meeting: "I have often referred to this time in my preaching in later years as the time that God in his sovereign grace met with me and brought me to the end of myself and thought fit to give me a share in the power of Pentecost."[7]

When Church returned to Gahini, he turned his efforts increasingly from doctoring to exhorting. For his part, Nsibambi soon resigned his post as a public health officer in favor of full-time teaching and ministry. Gradually the two of them brought others to see the spiritual world as they did—as requiring repentance, consecration, full surrender, and the power of the Holy Spirit. One of Nsibambi's friends, Yosiya Kinuka, initially resisted the revival message, but then in a small group meeting publicly repented of his sins of Christian formalism and pride. It was a practice that came to define the revival. Through a series of episodic conventions, informal gatherings and teaching opportunities (especially at schools), Church, Nsibambi and a growing circle of like-minded believers pursued their efforts with ever-greater intensity. The meeting of 1935 described at the start of this chapter galvanized even greater fervor. The number of those "on fire" (the *abaka*) increased steadily, the number of "the saved" *(balokole),* by leaps and bounds.

From the mid-1930s, the revival spread rapidly through the north of Uganda and into Kenya; it moved around Lake Victoria to Rwanda and Burundi; eventually it reached into Tanganyika. Through wide travels that Church later undertook with African colleagues, the revival message moved on to South Africa and several places outside of the African continent. But although Church was the most visible leader to Western eyes, his style of missionary activity was always deliberately cooperative. The practice of forming teams of workers—both mixed white and black as well as all-African—was from the start the chief vehicle of

---

[7]Church, *Quest for the Highest*, 66-68.

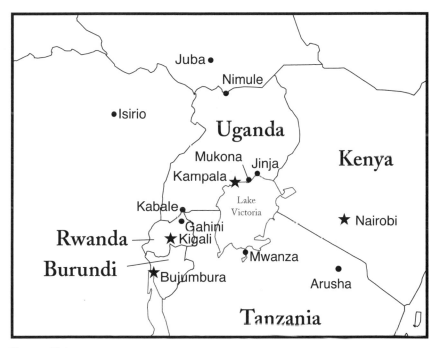

Figure 10.1

dissemination. Early meetings denounced racial pride and urged the *balokole* to seek reconciliation between Europeans and Africans. At one such event in 1937 whites and blacks alike publicly confessed their sins of racial pride. One African who attended said "I have never before seen any white man admit that he had any sins."[8]

The great enthusiasm of the *balokole* generated predictable difficulties. Missionaries worried about giving untrained Africans such free rein to their convictions. Anglican schools, where so much of the ferment began, were particularly stressed. In one famous incident from 1941 at Bishop Tucker Theological College in Mukona, Uganda, college officials thought the public confessions and assertive demands for repentance were getting out of hand. As a result, twenty-nine students were asked to leave. Their number included William Nagenda, who had gained renown as a revival preacher and would go on to become the revival's most effective agent in the following decades.

The Ugandan Anglican bishops, however, exercised as much flexibility as they could. As a result, the bishops—at this point still all British—succeeded in winning back most of the expelled students. Even more importantly, they were mostly successful in preventing the kind of schism that spawned Kenya's powerful independent churches. In Uganda, as a consequence, the Anglicans retained the revivalists and the revival fire within their own churches and schools. Anglican leaders also played a role in regularizing the emphases of the revival as "Five Pillars": repentance, faith, new birth, growth in grace and the power of the Holy Spirit.

Spiritual tensions also posed a threat to the revival's progress. In a pattern that repeated what had earlier transpired among pietists, evangelicals, Methodists and Pentecostals at various stages of European and American history, enthusiasts carried revival emphases into claims about the possibility, and then the realization, of perfection. A few who promoted perfectionistic teachings spun off to form their own new churches, but most were recalled by the revivals' main leaders to positions that balanced spiritual zeal and organizational loyalty.

---

[8]Shaw, "Hunger for Holiness," 30.

By the late 1940s, the revival was spreading through large conferences where numbers reached into the hundreds of thousands. Unlike earlier attempts at convening such mass meetings, these gatherings were planned, organized and conducted by an all-African leadership. Also unlike earlier attempts, these meetings were spectacularly successful. Into the 1950s and 1960s, the revival spread to more and more regions and came to influence more and more churches. Only the most determined of the African Independent Churches and only the mission churches most tightly tethered to British, European and now also American control remained immune to the revival influence.

During the 1950s, the last colonial decade, the *balokole* were beginning to exert a broader influence. When the region's Anglican churches started to appoint African bishops, veterans of the revival were first in line. This pattern was soon repeated in other churches making the transition to African leadership. In the turmoil that led up to independence for these East African nations, the revivalists remained relatively aloof, standing neither with the Mau-Mau and other aggressive advocates of political change nor with those in the mission churches that clung to the colonial order.

Only in the last years of the twentieth century did the revival begin to lose some of its influence in the region. Here again a pattern seen before in American history provided a precedent. When strongly Pentecostal and neo-Pentecostal groups began to make headway, it was obvious to all outside observers that they did so by laying special stress on common themes of the revival. But initiatives that might appear like small differences of emphasis concerning the power of the Holy Spirit have created fissures that clearly separate some of the new groups from the churches still strongly influenced by the revival.

The region's recent political history has witnessed legacies of the revival that reflect upon it both favorably and unfavorably. For civil society in Uganda and Kenya the revival's spiritual roots have borne beneficial fruit. The revival's strong commitment to fellowship, public repentance and the abasement of self have provided a solid spiritual base enabling leaders to act in public with remarkable courage and unusual integrity. In Uganda, under the bloody dictatorship of Idi Amin (1971-1979), *balokole* who had become leaders of the Anglican Church provided rare stability and forthright public leadership. For his pains in speaking truth to power, the Anglican Archbishop Janani Luwum was murdered in early 1977; after fleeing the country in the wake of this assassination, Bishop Festo Kivengere offered his powerful testimony in the United States and elsewhere. Even the current Ugandan president Yoweri Museveni was deeply touched as a young man by the East African revival, and his wife, Janet, remains identified with evangelical causes.[9]

In Kenya, somewhat later, the Anglican Archbishop David Gitari provided a notable defense of public justice under the corrupt regime of Daniel arap Moi and through the constitutional crises that followed. In these and other circumstances on a local level, a signal contribution from those touched by the revival has been to let Christian principles, standards of equity and a commitment to justice trump the ancestral tribal loyalties that in other circumstances have bloodied the region.

The bloodiest of those circumstances was the Rwandan genocide of 1994. For the Protestants involved, this horrific event testified to social and cultural weaknesses of the revival. A narrow use of Scripture and a conception of piety limited to personal holiness did not do much to check the upsurge of tribal strife that led to hundreds of thousands of deaths.

Yet Western comparisons, which are germane for the religious development of the revival, are also relevant for assessing its weaknesses. The revival's ardent form of self-abnegating and Spirit-filled Christianity has not yet succeeded in overcoming the tribal antagonisms that European colonization exacerbated. Yet an African looking at the dreadful carnage of Europe's twentieth-century world wars, or at the sorry record of racial strife throughout all of United States history, might observe that things in Africa have never been as violent as that nor that contradictory to the Christian principles supposedly guiding

---

[9]See Kevin Ward, "The Church of Uganda amidst Conflict," in *Religion and Politics in East Africa: The Period Since Independence,* ed. Holger Hansen and Michael Twaddle (Athens: Ohio University Press, 1995).

the West's churched population for more than a millennium. In addition, African observers could point to the record of bishops Luwum, Kivengere, Gitari and still others, and argue plausibly that their contributions rank with the most honorable public actions to be found anywhere in the globe over the last half century.

AFRICAN OR WESTERN?

But what of the revival regarded in spiritual and religious terms? Was it merely a Western import, or did the East African Revival represent a genuinely African appropriation of Christian faith?

One way to answer is to focus on the many obviously Western elements that permeated the revival from its beginning and right up to the early twenty-first century. To the Rwanda mission Joe Church brought Keswick spirituality, the Scofield Reference Bible and the practices of Moral Re-Armament along with his Western medicines and Western medical training. In addition, his self-conscious model for much of his revival activity was Charles Finney, the dynamic American evangelist of the middle third of the nineteenth century. In March 1939, Church conducted a two-week, 1700-mile series of meetings that took him, his wife Decima and William Nagenda through southern Sudan, Uganda, Congo, Rwanda, then back to Kabale in Uganda. At each stop the three were able either to fan the fires of revival already underway or turn new initiates to the repentance, confessions and serious commitment that already marked so many other places in the region. As Church drove from place to place, the revival team passed the miles with William Nagenda reading aloud from an often-reprinted book by Charles Finney that had first appeared in 1835. It was Finney's *Revivals of Religion*, a volume that set out the message and the techniques that Finney had used in his noteworthy labors in the United States.[10] With chapters like "How to Promote a Revival," "Be Filled with the Spirit," "Means to be Used with Sinners," "Hindrances to Revivals," "Instructions to Converts," "Backsliders in Heart" and "Growth in Grace," Finney's volume not only filled the miles but seemed to link evangelism in the

---

[10]Church, *Quest for the Highest*, 166.

colonial population of twentieth-century Africa with evangelism in the rising cities of nineteenth-century America. What could be more obvious than the decisive direction provided to a rising generation of earnest African evangelicals by these standard guides from the evangelical and fundamentalist worlds of Britain and America?

Yet the fact that great numbers of Africans became enthusiasts for the kind of Protestantism practiced by Western evangelicals does not by itself mean that these Western influences were in any simple sense dictating to East Africa. If Africans chose these emphases for themselves, then perhaps their own decision-making was center-stage. And if these emphases came from channels like Joe Church, who was deeply committed to Africans directing the work of African ministry, there is even more reason to regard the revival as an African event.

Not so fast, might be the response. Sugarcoated and softly enforced manipulation is still manipulation. Yes, perhaps, but if one supplements a look at the transit of some Western practices to Africa with closer attention to African circumstances, there is even more reason to move away from conclusions about "manipulation" toward a much more complicated picture of Western-African relationships.

In one very important particular it is relatively obvious why the form of Christianity that East Africans embraced by the hundreds of thousands from the 1920s onward was a Christianity that spoke so powerfully to them. From the late nineteenth century, traditional African society, with its strong sense of family and "blood" ties, fell under devastating pressure. The European scramble for Africa destabilized domestic and tribal institutions that had already been put to the test by slavery and local tribal conflicts. The imposition of colonialism, with its artificial geography and its new authority from the center, exacerbated that strain. In this setting, a religion that featured a new kind of life-changing and life-satisfying teamwork—a new religion that showed how a new spiritual family could be formed by trust in "the blood of Christ"—was a religion with resources well adapted to the situation of early-colonial African society.

This way of analyzing the appeal of Keswick-type spirituality and the practices of Moral Re-Armament is not meant to deny that powerful spiritual forces have been at work in East Africa for nearly a century. It suggests, rather, that a message, which had enjoyed a powerful appeal in Britain and America when these societies were marked by their own dislocations, might logically have a similar appeal in other societies when they experience similar circumstances.

More specifically, in at least some of the places where the revival took hold, ancient but distressed African practices provided a perfect cultural preparation for what followed. In a careful study of Kikuyu Anglicanism, for instance, John Karanja notes that "the practice of public confession . . . suited Kikuyu religious consciousness" because "confession was an integral part of Kikuyu religion and culture." Karanja points out that in traditional Kikuyu culture public confession had been "administered to remove *thahu* and to effect physical healing. The ceremony of *gutahiko* (symbolic vomiting) was conducted by a medicine-man to whom the client disclosed all his misdeeds." Karanja speculates, moreover, that one reason for the more rapid advance of Protestant-type groups over Catholicism among the Kikuyu was the seamless glide from traditional practice to revival practice: not private confession to a priest, but public confession to the whole assembly continued directly, in a new Christian form, what had been practiced in the ancient Kikuyu religion.[11]

When viewed, therefore, from the perspective of the African participants in African circumstances, the East African Revival looks more and more like an African event. The American anthropologist, Brian Howell, has studied a similar situation in another location and come to a similar conclusion. Howell's subject is Protestantism in the modern Philippines, including the Southern Baptist churches in the Philippine north. Howell's research reveals a Filipino church where the beliefs, practices and mores encouraged by American missionaries are unusually prominent. His conclusion, however, is not that these Southern Baptist Filipinos are being manipulated by their American missionary colleagues. Rather, Howell concludes that for their own local reasons the Filipino Southern Baptists have chosen to

---

[11]Karanja, *Founding an African Faith*, 251.

accept the form of Southern Baptist religion. They look amazingly like Southern Baptists from south of the American Mason-Dixon Line, but they remain Filipinos in the self-direction they provide for their form of Christianity.[12]

If the East African Revival is assessed with similar attention to local conditions and local choices, it is clear that Howell's analysis works as well in the African case as for the subjects of his own research. Following this form of analysis also shows why the African contributions to the current crises of worldwide Anglicanism make much more sense as indigenously African contributions than as interventions orchestrated by Western conservatives. In East Africa, revival produced a passionate evangelical religion that stayed within mainline denominations. It featured an emphasis on fellowship where common decision-making and cooperative teamwork was of the essence. And it arose in a twentieth-century context where issues of sexuality were always critical for Christian self-definition, first with respect to polygamy and female circumcision, and then in responding to the HIV/AIDS crisis. When looking at African Christianity from within Africa, nothing makes more sense than the way the East African bishops have taken part in the recent history of the Anglican Communion.

The East African Revival represents, in sum, a distinctly African chapter in the recent history of Christianity. In an era of extraordinary political and social upheaval, Christianity assumed an African shape, even as Africans followed their own initiatives in embracing salient aspects of Christian faith as practiced in the Western world.

What did the East African Revival look like and what kind of Christianity did it become? At a glance, the revival appeared to be an unlikely blend of Wesleyan-Anglican theology, Pentecostal fervor and African passion. Miracles happened. People were healed, saw prophetic visions, spoke in tongues, sang all night, did battle with evil spirits and discussed sermons long into the night. Often they gathered

---

[12]Brian Howell, "Globalization as a Local Process: Philippine Baptist Identity at the End of the Twentieth Century," in *Baptist Identities: International Studies from the Seventeenth to the Twentieth Centuries*, ed. Ian Randall, Toilo Pilli and Anthony Cross (London: Paternoster, 2006), 257-74.

before dawn to pray. They sang and sometimes danced their worship with great passion. They confessed their sins to one another. They studied the Bible. They shared the gospel with all who would listen—and some who wouldn't. And much of this took place as part of Anglican worship and within Anglican ecclesiastical guidelines. It was, from the outside, a strange mix of the local and the global. From the inside, it all made sense.

Reflections

THE MAIN POINT OF THIS BOOK IS THAT AMERICAN CHRISTI-anity is important for the world primarily because the world is coming more and more to look like America. Therefore, the way that Christianity developed in the American environment helps to explain the way Christianity is developing in many parts of the world. But correlation is not causation: the fact that globalization and other factors have created societies that resemble in many ways what Americans experienced in the frontier period of their history does not mean that Americans are dictating to the world. It means, instead, that understanding American patterns provides insight for what has been happening elsewhere in the world.[1] The actions of American Christians are obviously of great importance in the world, but American actions by no means dominate or simply ordain what is happening elsewhere.

If this general picture is even partially correct, a number of other things remain to be said. This last chapter does not attempt a conclu-

---

[1]I would like to thank the student who in a Wheaton College class uttered the "correlation is not causation" phrase, but I'm afraid I've forgotten who he or she was.

sion as such. Far too many momentous developments have been taking place in the recent world history of Christianity, and far too much about the future depends upon events and circumstances that cannot be predicted, to allow for a clean summary or a neat conclusion. But it is still possible to reflect on the complex history of this last period in world Christian history and so move beyond the recital of events to assessment and analysis.

THE ENDURING CHARACTER AND ENDURING ATTRACTION OF THE CHRISTIAN FAITH

In light of its recent history, Christianity itself appears more and more as an essentially pluralistic and crosscultural faith. As Lamin Sanneh has recently phrased it, the teaching of Jesus and his apostles showed that "territoriality [had] ceased to be a requirement of faith. . . . Converts [from wherever they came] were deemed to have permanent tenure."[2] In its very earliest decades, the gospel message, which appeared first in a Semitic milieu, moved eastward into Asia, southwestward into Africa, and northwestward into Europe. Immediately those who turned to Christ in these "new" regions were at home in the faith. When they became believers, Christianity itself became Asian, European and African. And so it has gone for nearly two thousand years. The agents that communicate Christianity to places that had not before known the gospel might come from far away; their understanding of the faith might be defined by cultural patterns from those far away places. But once Christianity is rooted in someplace new, the faith itself also takes on something from that new place.

Of course, when Christianity is rooted in someplace new, it also challenges, reforms and humanizes the cultural values of that new place. Andrew Walls has aptly described this twofold process as combining "indigenization" and "pilgrimage." The gospel comes to each person and to all peoples exactly where they are. You do not have to stop being an American, a Japanese, a German or a Terra del Fuegian in order to become a Christian. Rather, Americans, Japanese, Germans,

<hr>

[2]Lamin Sanneh, *Disciples of All Nations: Pillars of World Christianity* (New York: Oxford University Press, 2008), 7, 10.

Terra del Fuegians or anyone else will find rich resources in Christianity that are perfectly fitted for their own cultural situations. Yet even as the gospel dignifies individual cultures, by entering into all of them so particularly, it also calls all believers together to a pilgrim journey, and that journey inevitably involves rejecting some aspects of the native culture. The gospel that legitimates the particular upholds the universal. The gospel that communicates dignity to each believer from whatever culture calls each Christian to join all others in praising the universal rule of God in Christ. Believers will (in fact, must) worship in different ways. But believers together worship the one God revealed in the Son who fills all things.[3]

Accidents of history sometime obscure the pilgrim side of this twofold reality. The long dominance of Christianity in Europe; the extraordinary power of Christendom as a cultural, political, artistic and social ideal; the sustaining presence of the Roman Catholic Church as the world's oldest continuously functioning international institution; and the economic and political influence of Europe around the globe since the late fifteenth century—all can leave the impression that there is something intrinsically European about the Christian faith. Generations of Europeans sailing off into the world at large certainly acted as if they thought so, while generations of non-Europeans understandably received the same impression.

Similarly, in the recent past, the adolescent exuberance of the United States as the world's newest global power has often left the same impression. Where the United States has gone, Christianity defined as an American religion has gone before, accompanied or followed closely thereafter.

The impression that Christianity in its essence is either European or American is, however, simply false. Christianity began as Jewish; before it was European, it was North African, Syrian, Egyptian and Indian. While in recent history it has indeed been American, it has also been Chilean, Albanian, Fijian and Chinese. The gospel belongs to every one in every culture; it belongs to no one in any one culture in particular.

---

[3]Andrew F. Walls, *The Missionary Movement in Christian History: Studies in the Transmission of Faith* (Maryknoll, N.Y.: Orbis, 1996), 26-36.

And how can that be? One who believes in Christ can only answer that the Lord Jesus is the Savior of all who trust in him (Jn 3:16-17), the Light of the whole world (Jn 9:5), the one who embodies the will of God that all should come to repentance (2 Pet 3:9). The extraordinary diversity of cultures in which Christianity has taken root and continues to take root depends upon a universal theology. Because the appeal of Christianity is universal—because individuals, families, clans, groups and societies from anywhere and everywhere have been drawn to God by cords of divine love—Christianity by its very character is poised to meet individuals, families, clans, groups and societies where they are. It is by its nature a religion of nearly infinite flexibility because it has been revealed in a person of absolutely infinite love. The intrinsic appeal of that love to people of every culture is the reason for the cultural diversity of Christianity in its past and at the present.

Given what Christianity is and why it has enjoyed such a wide appeal, it follows that all historical and geographical concentrations of Christian faith are important for illustrating various special strengths (and weaknesses) of a general process. They are never important for representing a last, final or definite expression of Christianity, since the process that made the faith so important in a particular time or region is the same process that makes it so important in other times and for other regions. There can be no denying that European Christendom and recent American Christianity have been powerful instantiations of the faith. Similarly, however, there can be no denying that instantiations that are just as powerful have already appeared in other places at other times, and may do so again in, say, sub-Saharan Africa, post-communist China or a Latin America transformed by revival.

THE EFFECTS OF AMERICAN HISTORY ON AMERICAN CONCEPTIONS OF CHRISTIANITY

Some aspects of American history, especially as experienced by Protestants in the United States, make it difficult to grasp the inherently multicultural, pluralistic character of the one true faith. In particular, thinking that minimizes the cultural contexts for religious actions has been common throughout American history. A conception of religion that does not see how the particular shape of American culture has influenced the character of American Christianity is perhaps especially strong among evangelical believers. In evangelical circles, for example, it is common to hear assertions about separating "real Christianity" from its merely "cultural expressions." Some things are true Christianity; others are "just culture."

To many looking on from the outside, however, this conception of true Christianity as easily separable from culture is itself a product of distinct patterns in American history.[4] The nature of American experience, for example, has tended to obscure the disruption that throughout most of human history accompanies religious conversion. That same experience has also promoted ideas about how easy it is to transform societies through voluntaristic means.

But believing that conversion can take place without a whole lot of social or cultural disruption or that social transformation can take place through the simple aggregation of individual effort are beliefs that reflect a distinctive American history. For the middle colonies from the seventeenth century and for the whole United States from its independence in the 1770s, Caucasian men have operated in a loose social space with extraordinary opportunities for making personal choices and for acting upon those choices. More recently that same open space has been opened for white women and many new immigrants, especially those from Asia. The fluidity of American society, the huge expanse of American territory, and the relatively light hand of American government (indeed, before the Civil War of the 1860s, the virtually invisible hand of American government)—these circumstances have offered Americans more latitude for creating their own institutions of religious and civil society than almost any people elsewhere ever enjoyed in human history.

The stresses in American experience on a particular type of conversion and a particular type of voluntary action are by no means unique to the United States, since they have existed in many other places. What has been singular in America is the open social order where

---

[4]Patterns of interaction between evangelical Protestants and American history are explored in Mark A. Noll, *The Scandal of the Evangelical Mind* (Grand Rapids: Eerdmans, 1994).

converted individuals are afforded wide space to refashion themselves as a result of conversion and where voluntary activity by the converted (as well as by groups driven by other motives) has been able to accomplish extraordinary results. Given the American experience of what has been possible for Christian believers, it is no surprise that American Christians have often expected the arrival of Christianity in other parts of the world to produce results that look pretty much like Christianity in the United States.

The American tendency, especially among evangelicals, to reduce true religion to conversion, which requires only choice to accomplish, and activistic social engagement, which requires only voluntary choice, represents a simplification of both Christianity and human experience. This picture of conversion was possible in American history only because most Americans enjoyed the legacy of Christendom with its assumptions about Christian life and practice. That life and practice may have grown cold and the structures of Christendom might have fallen away, but the basic Christian orientation remained in place for a very long time. The picture of voluntarism as the golden key to effective social action was possible only because another unusual set of circumstances in the United States provided a social space that was nearly empty by most world standards and an ideal of political order that grew out of an unusual commitment to democracy.

The importance of this simplified American picture to world events has been striking. This vision of Christianity stripped down to conversion and voluntary activity has been liable to exploitation for the purposes of colonization, sometimes directly through political and military power, more often indirectly through economic and cultural influence. But it is not a picture that leads naturally to deliberate imperialism. Americans have often been perceived as throwing their weight around in the world, when in their own eyes they are just trying to help others out. The reality usually lies between these perceptions: American Christians have often been pushy and unthinking when imposing American norms on others, but compared to historical European or Asian imperialism, American influence abroad has often been applied with relatively few strings attached. Thus, American missionary activity has never been apolitical, or culture-free, or simply spiritual, even if American believers sometimes conceive of their mission work in those terms. By the same token, however, the cultural and imperial impositions of American missionary activity have been relatively light, especially by comparison with the other great empires of history.

The missionary style that has been such a strong feature of America's presence in the world acquired special relevance over the course of the twentieth century as more and more non-Western regions evolved in directions roughly similar to American society and culture. Few places have enjoyed the open geography of early American history, but many have experienced uprooted social, economic, intellectual and cultural conditions that provide parallel opportunities to what Americans enjoyed earlier in their history. Where in other parts of the world social conditions prevail that, for whatever reason, offer anything even remotely resembling the American experiences of open space for personal, voluntaristic agency, in those places voluntaristic and conversionistic Christianity is now exerting a tremendous force.

THE PLACE OF WESTERN MISSIONARIES

The interpretation I am offering for world Christian history might seem to be an anti-missionary interpretation. In some sense, it probably is. Where the impression prevails that the fate of Christianity depends upon missionaries from any one part of the world bringing the faith to other parts of the world, the actual realities of Christian history are obscured. As the cascade of scholarship on world Christianity continues to expand (for individual titles, see the "Guide to Further Reading"), a common pattern becomes clearer for the great diversity of world Christian expansion. There is first contact with the gospel (often from missionaries), and there are very often early efforts at evangelization and at humanitarian aid (usually from missionaries). But the actual movement from Christian beachhead to functioning Christian community is almost always the work of local Christians. Korean revivalists; African prophets, catechists and Bible women; Indian preachers and bishops; Latin American priests, Pentecostal preachers and cell group leaders; South Sea Islander chiefs and teachers; imprisoned Chi-

nese apostles—these are the human agents that over the last century
and a half have transformed Christianity from a Western to a genuinely
world religion. When Christianity is understood as always a cultural
force (instead of just a religion of personal conversion) and always a
cultural expression, then it becomes obvious why the ones who really
know local cultures have the greatest impact in those cultures as wit-
nesses for Christ.

But if this interpretation might seem to denigrate the place of missionaries, it does so only if missionary service is depicted unrealistically.
In the New Testament, it is crystal clear that crosscultural communication (missions) does require proclamation, preaching, the bringing of
the good news. Romans 10:14-15 is a classic passage underscoring these
realities. What the New Testament does not teach is that the ones who
proclaim the message in new cultural settings are responsible for how
the churches develop in those new cultures. Rather, as the journeys of
the Apostle Paul depicted in the book of Acts seem to indicate, the
proclaimers (like Paul) are eager to pass on local leadership to local
leaders. They are eager, in modern parlance, to let the ones who know
the local culture do the job of inculturating the faith.

In this picture, missionary service remains of critical importance,
but not because missionaries are intended to exercise a God-like authority in shaping responses to gospel proclamation. Rather, they remain critical to the world Christian picture because they are the ones
called to begin a process that succeeds fully—that succeeds in accord
with properly Christian understandings of the God-given diversity of
cultures—only when the missionaries get out of the way.

PARTNERSHIP

Lamin Sanneh ends his recent account of world Christian dynamics
with an arresting statement:

> The fact that disadvantaged peoples and their cultures are buoyed by
> new waves of conversion has created alignments of global scope at the
> margins of power and privilege. The paradigm nature of the realign-
> ment compels a fundamental stocktaking of Christianity's frontier
> awakening, and an imperative of partnership with it. When opportu-

nity knocks the wise will build bridges while the timorous will build dams. It is a new day.[5]

This book has mostly explored American connections with "the new day" that Sanneh evokes. It should not end, however, without underscoring what he calls the "imperative of partnership."

It is increasingly clear that all true expressions of Christianity, like politics in the famous American saying, are local. When the Christian faith takes real root, it takes real root in particular places and works in and through the cultural values of those places to restore fellowship with God, undergird functioning churches, and do the work of Christ in the world. Agents from outside that culture may play important roles in assisting, or hindering, Christian maturation, but Christianity has to be local or it can barely be called Christianity.

Yet the clear message of Scripture, reflected in various ways in the defining documents of almost all Christian traditions, is that all believers wherever they are found make up a universal entity. Believers in one local cultural expression of Christian faith are linked to all others in their local cultural settings because all are joined to Christ. This linkage, moreover, is much more than just a jigsaw puzzle where the pieces constitute a mosaic but touch only those pieces that are in closest proximity. Rather, the great image from Scripture is of the body of Christ where circulation (meaning assistance), a unified nervous system (meaning communication), and coordinated muscular exertion (meaning common action) are essential.

The image of Christ's body makes it possible to think again about the American place in world Christianity. Regardless of which part of the body one would like to assign the American Christian community, that part of the body cannot be viewed as more important than any other part; neither can it be thought to function without necessary dependence on the rest. The beauty of the body image for world Christianity is its mutuality. As all share in Christ, all share in each other. Every body part, no matter how prominent, needs every other one, no matter how obscure. Some will carry out more visible functions, but none can get along without the others.

[5]Sanneh, *Disciples of All Nations*, 287.

In world Christian terms, some national expressions of Christian faith may seem more prominent than others, but all are in fact equally necessary for the well-being of all, and all are equally dependent upon the rest. This picture suggests that some goods may continue to flow predominately from the West to the rest of the world—perhaps, for at least the foreseeable future, money, formal education or expertise in managing the opportunities and crises of globalization. But it also suggests that other goods should be expected to flow in the other direction—perhaps lessons on experiencing Christ's peace when there is no money, instruction on how at the same time to love and confront members of other faiths, reminders of how the living exist in close proximity to the dead, or practical examples in overcoming historical antagonisms through the direct power of the Holy Spirit.

For American churches to participate in the universal body of Christ in ways that reflect the deepest realities of that body, it will be necessary to discard two false notions—both Western paternal benevolence in which the instinct is to think that unless Americans do it, it will not get done, and also Western hegemonic imperialism whereby all the evils of the world are laid at the feet of American-dominated multinationals or mission agencies. Once those delusions are set aside, practices of partnership drawing on genuine Christian realities may flourish.

THE PURPOSE OF THE GOSPEL

Scripture comes alive with new force when it is read as the book of God for all believers everywhere, as well as the book of God that speaks most directly to me in my particular time and place. Throughout Western Christian history, the message of the book of Isaiah was seen as speaking so strongly about the Messiah who was to come that Isaiah was often called "the evangelical prophet." As it was in former days of European Christendom, so it is in our day of world Christianity.

On the one side, the prophet is unremitting in the standard of righteousness he holds up for all peoples and the consequences that fall universally where that standard is violated. The passage at the start of chapter 34 is not atypical:

> Draw near, O nations, to hear;
>> O peoples, give heed!
> Let the earth hear, and all that fills it;
>> the world, and all that comes from it.
> For the Lord is enraged against all the nations,
>> and furious against all their hoardes;
>>> he has doomed them, has given them over for slaughter. (Is 34:1-2 NRSV)

More often, however, Isaiah's message to "the nations" comes from the other side. It is one that, even as it values Israel as the special people of God, shows that Jewish chosenness is a bridge to God's favor for all peoples:

> In days to come
>> the mountain of the LORD's house
> shall be established as the highest of the mountains,
>> and shall be raised above the hills;
> all the nations shall stream to it.
>> Many peoples shall come and say,
> "Come, let us go up to the mountain of the LORD,
>> to the house of the God of Jacob;
> that he may teach us his ways
>> and that we may walk in his paths." (Is 2:2-3 NRSV)

> On this mountain the LORD of hosts will make for all peoples
>> a feast of rich food, a feast of well-aged wines,
>> of rich food filled with marrow, of well-aged wines strained clear.
> And he will destroy on this mountain
>> the shroud that is cast over all peoples,
>> the sheet that is spread over all nations;
>> he will swallow up death forever. (Is 25:6-8 NRSV)

> For darkness shall cover the earth,
>> and thick darkness the peoples;
> but the LORD will arise upon you,
>> and his glory will appear over you.
> Nations shall come to your light,
>> and kings to the brightness of your dawn. (Is 60:2-3 NRSV)

I am coming to gather all nations and tongues; and they shall come and shall see my glory. . . . They shall bring all your kindred from all the nations as an offering to the LORD, on horses, and in chariots, and in litters, and on mules, and on dromedaries, to my holy mountain Jerusalem, says the LORD. . . . And I will also take some of them as priests and as Levites, says the LORD. (Is 66:18-21 NRSV)

The luxuriant diversity of transport that in Isaiah's prophecy brings "all nations and tongues" to worship the Lord in Jerusalem is a stepping stone to the narratives of the New Testament. Jesus' ministry to the Syro-Phoenician woman and the Samaritan woman at the well provided a foundation. On the day of Pentecost the gift of tongues, which has inspired Bible translators right to the present day, was on full display as a sign of the essentially multicultural character of the faith. The missionary journeys in Acts that saw so many from such various tribes and peoples respond to the gospel carried this message further. And it received renewed expression in John's Apocalypse that draws the New Testament to a close. One of the most forceful of such statements is also a good passage with which to end this book.[6] It is the vision right at conclusion of the book of Revelation that exalts "the Lord God, the Almighty and the Lamb" as providing all the illumination that is necessary in the New Jerusalem: "the glory of God is its light, and its lamp is the Lamb." Immediately after describing this Light at the center, the passage moves on to the effects of God's saving works for the world as a whole: "The nations will walk by its light, and the kings of the earth will bring their glory into it" (Rev 21:22-24 NRSV).

This vision of divine fulfillment picks up Isaiah's theme about the kings of the earth even as it speaks graphically about the universal outreach of the gospel. The passage also hints at the sanctification of the world's diverse cultures. The kings—or, we might expand, the cultures of the world—with their glory will enter the heavenly city. For Americans who read this stirring account of the fulfillment to which the whole world points, it should be enough to imagine that one of those "kings" will come from the White House, but only one.

---

[6]I thank Richard Mouw for leading me to this passage with this interpretation.

GUIDE TO FURTHER READING

I began this book by saying that the new shape of world Christianity demands a new history of Christianity. On the shelves of libraries and at booksellers the new history is in fact already to hand, even if it still has not yet reached a broader public. The books cited here only begin to scratch the surface of the burgeoning number of titles that are now available.

Reference Works
Barrett, David. *World Christian Encyclopedia*. New York: Oxford University Press, 1982.

Barrett, David, George T. Kurian and Todd M. Johnson. *World Christian Encyclopedia*. 2 vols. 2nd ed. New York: Oxford University Press, 2001.

Barrett, David, and Todd M. Johnson. *World Christian Trends, AD 20–AD 2200: Interpreting the Annual Christian Megacensus*. Pasadena: William Carey Library, 2001.

International Bulletin of Missionary Research [this quarterly journal is the premier periodical in English for research in world Christianity].

Johnstone, Patrick, and Jason Mandryk. *Operation World: 21st Century Edition*. Carlisle, U.K.: Paternoster, 2001.

Weber, Linda J., and Dotsey Welliver. *Mission Handbook, 2007-2009: U.S. and Canadian Ministries Overseas*. Wheaton, Ill.: EMIS, 2007.

General Works
Anderson, Allan. *An Introduction to Pentecostalism: Global Charismatic Christianity*. New York: Cambridge University Press, 2004.

Bamat, Thomas, and Jean-Paul Wiest, eds. *Popular Catholicism in a World Church: Seven Case Studies in Inculturation*. Maryknoll, N.Y.: Orbis, 1999.

Coleman, Simon. *The Globalisation of Charismatic Christianity: Spreading the Gospel of Prosperity*. New York: Cambridge University Press, 2000.

Freston, Paul. *Evangelicals and Politics in Asia, Africa and Latin America*. New York: Cambridge University Press, 2001.

———. *Protestant Political Parties: A Global Survey*. Burlington, Vt.: Ashgate, 2004.

Hastings, Adrian, ed. *A World History of Christianity*. Grand Rapids: Eerdmans, 1999.

Hutchinson, Mark, and Ogbu Kalu, eds. *A Global Faith: Essays on Evangelization and Globalization*. Sydney: Centre for the Study of Australian Christianity, 1998.

Jenkins, Philip. *God's Continent: Christianity, Islam, and Europe's Religious Crisis*. New York: Oxford University Press, 2007.

———. *The New Faces of Christianity: Believing the Bible in the Global South*. New York: Oxford University Press, 2006.

———. *The Next Christendom: The Coming of Global Christianity*. New York: Oxford University Press, 1999.

Lewis, Donald, ed. *Christianity Reborn: The Global Expansion of Evangelicalism in the Twentieth Century*. Grand Rapids: Eerdmans, 2004.

Martin, David. *Pentecostalism: The World Their Parish*. Oxford: Blackwell, 2002.

McLeod, Hugh, ed. *The Cambridge History of Christianity, 9: World Christianities, c. 1914–c. 2000*. New York: Cambridge University Press, 2006.

Parratt, John, ed. *An Introduction to Third World Theologies*. New York: Cambridge University Press, 2004.

Porter, Andrew, ed. *The Imperial Horizon of British Protestant Missions, 1980-1914*. Grand Rapids: Eerdmans, 2003.

———. *Religion Versus Empire? British Protestant Missionaries and Overseas Expansion, 1700-1914*. New York: Manchester University Press, 2004.

Sanneh, Lamin. *Disciples of All Nations: Pillars of World Christianity*. New York: Oxford University Press, 2008.

————. *Translating the Message: The Missionary Impact on Culture.* Maryknoll, N.Y.: Orbis, 1989.

————. *Whose Religion Is Christianity? The Gospel Beyond the West.* Grand Rapids: Eerdmans, 2003.

Stanley, Brian, ed. *Missions, Nationalism, and the End of Empire.* Grand Rapids: Eerdmans, 2003.

Walls, Andrew F. *The Cross-Cultural Process in Christian History.* Maryknoll, N.Y.: Orbis, 2002.

————. *The Missionary Movement in Christian History.* Maryknoll, N.Y.: Orbis, 1996.

Ward, Kevin. *A History of Global Anglicanism.* New York: Cambridge University Press, 2006.

Ward, Kevin, and Brian Stanley, eds. *The Church Mission Society and World Christianity, 1799-1999.* Grand Rapids: Eerdmans, 2000.

Africa

Anderson, Allan. *African Reformation: African Initiated Christianity in the Twentieth Century.* Trenton, N.J.: Africa World Press, 2002.

Bediako, Kwame. *Christianity in Africa: The Revival of a Non-Western Religion.* Maryknoll, N.Y.: Orbis, 1995.

Daneel, Martinus L. *African Earthkeepers: Wholistic Interfaith Mission.* Maryknoll, N.Y.: Orbis, 2001.

Gifford, Paul. *African Christianity: Its Public Role.* Bloomington: Indiana University Press, 1998.

Hastings, Adrian. *A History of African Christianity, 1950-1974.* New York: Cambridge University Press, 1979.

Hastings, Adrian. *The Church in Africa, 1450-1950.* New York: Oxford University Press, 1994.

Isichei, Elizabeth. *A History of Christianity in Africa.* Grand Rapids: Eerdmans, 1995.

Kalu, Ogbu U. *African Pentecostalism: An Introduction.* New York: Oxford University Press, 2008.

————. *Power, Poverty, and Prayer: The Challenge of Poverty and Pluralism in African Christianity, 1960-1996.* Frankfurt: Peter Lang, 2000.

————, ed. *African Christianity: An African Story*. Trenton, N.J.: Africa World Press, 2007.

Kollman, Paul V. *The Evangelization of Slaves and Catholic Origins in Eastern Africa*. Maryknoll, N.Y.: Orbis, 2005.

Peel, John Y. *Religious Encounter and the Making of the Yoruba*. Bloomington: Indiana University Press, 2001.

Ranger, Terence O., ed. *Evangelical Christianity and Democracy in Africa*. New York: Oxford University Press, 2008.

Sanneh, Lamin. *Abolitionists Abroad: American Blacks and the Making of Modern West Africa*. New Haven: Yale University Press, 1999.

Shaw, Mark. *The Kingdom of God in Africa: A Short History of African Christianity*. Grand Rapids: Baker, 1996.

Stinton, Diane B. *Jesus of Africa: Voices of Contemporary African Christology*. Maryknoll, N.Y.: Orbis, 2004.

Sundkler, Bengt, and Christopher Steed. *A History of the Church in Africa*. New York: Cambridge University Press, 2000.

Asia (general and excluding China and India)

Breward, Ian. *A History of the Churches in Australasia*. New York: Oxford University Press, 2001.

Lumsdaine, David Halloran, ed. *Evangelical Christianity and Democracy in Asia*. New York: Oxford University Press, 2009.

Moffett, Samuel Hugh. *A History of Christianity in Asia: Vol. II, 1500–1900*. Maryknoll, N.Y.: Orbis, 2005.

Park, Chung-Shin. *Protestantism and Politics in Korea*. Seattle: University of Washington Press, 2003.

Robbins, Joel. *Becoming Sinners: Christianity and Moral Torment in a Papua New Guinea Society*. Berkeley: University of California Press, 2004.

China

Aikman, David. *Jesus in Beijing: How Christianity Is Transforming China and Changing the Global Balance of Power*. Washington, D.C.: Regnery, 2003.

Austin, Alvyn. *China's Millions: The China Inland Mission and Late Qing Society, 1832-1905*. Grand Rapids: Eerdmans, 2007.

Bays, Daniel, ed. *Christianity in China: From the Eighteenth Century to the Present*. Stanford: Stanford University Press, 1996.

Brockey, Liam Matthew. *Journey to the East: The Jesuit Mission to China, 1579-1724*. Cambridge, Mass.: Harvard University Press, 2007.

Charbonnier, Jean-Pierre. *Christians in China, A.D. 600 to 2000*. San Francisco: Ignatius, 2007.

Dunch, Ryan. *Fuzhou Protestants and the Making of a Modern China*. New Haven: Yale University Press, 2001.

Harvey, Thomas Alan. *Acquainted with Grief: Wang Mingdao's Stand for the Persecuted Church in China*. Grand Rapids: Brazos, 2002.

Kindrop, Jason, and Carol Lee Hamrin, eds. *God and Caesar in China: Policy Implications of Church-State Tensions*. Washington, D.C.: Brookings Institution Press, 2004.

Madsen, Richard. *China's Catholics*. Berkeley: University of California Press, 1998.

Wickeri, Philip I.. *Reconstructing Christianity in China: K. H. Ting and the Chinese Church*. Maryknoll, N.Y.: Orbis, 2007.

Yeo, K. K. *Chairman Mao Meets the Apostle Paul: Christianity, Communism, and the Hope of China*. Grand Rapids: Brazos, 2002.

India

Bergunder, Michael. *The South India Pentecostal Movement in the Twentieth Century*. Grand Rapids: Eerdmans, 2008.

Brown, Judith M., and Robert Eric Frykenberg, eds. *Christians, Cultural Interactions, and India's Religious Traditions*. Grand Rapids: Eerdmans, 2002.

Cox, Jeffrey. *Imperial Faultlines: Christianity and Colonial Power in India, 1818-1940*. Stanford: Stanford University Press, 2002.

Frykenberg, Robert Eric. *Christianity in India: From Beginnings to the Present*. New York: Oxford University Press, 2008.

———, ed. *Pandita Ramabai's America*. Grand Rapids: Eerdmans, 2003.

Frykenberg, Robert Eric, and Alaine M. Low, eds. *Christians and Missionaries in India: Cross-Cultural Communication since 1500, With*

Special Reference to Caste, Conversion, and Colonialism. Grand Rapids: Eerdmans, 2003.

Harper, Susan Billington. *In the Shadow of the Mahatma: Bishop V. S. Azariah and the Travails of Christianity in British India.* Grand Rapids: Eerdmans, 2000.

Mallampalli, Chandra. *Christians and Public Life in Colonial South India, 1863-1937: Contending with Marginality.* London: Routledge/Curzon, 2004.

Pickett, J. Waskom. *Christian Mass Movements in India.* New York: Abingdon, 1933.

Latin America

Bonino, José Míguez. *Faces of Latin American Protestantism.* Grand Rapids: Eerdmans, 1997.

Bowen, Kurt. *Evangelism and Apostasy: The Evolution and Impact of Evangelicals in Modern Mexico.* Toronto and Kingston: McGill-Queen's University Press, 1996.

Chestnut, R. Andrew. *Competitive Spirits: Latin America's New Religious Economy.* New York: Oxford University Press, 2003.

Freston, Paul, ed. *Evangelical Christianity and Democracy in Latin America.* New York: Oxford University Press, 2008.

Gill, Anthony. *Rendering Unto Caesar: The Catholic Church and the State in Latin America.* Chicago: University of Chicago Press, 1998.

González, Ondina E., and Justo L. González. *Christianity in Latin America: A History.* New York: Cambridge University Press, 2008.

Martin, David. *Tongues of Fire: The Explosion of Protestantism in Latin America.* Oxford: Blackwell, 1990.

Rowland, Christopher, ed. *The Cambridge Companion to Liberation Theology.* New York: Cambridge University Press, 1999.

Sigmund, Paul E., ed. *Religious Freedom and Evangelization in Latin America.* Maryknoll, N.Y.: Orbis, 1999.

Index